£70

CW01508573

We would each be half owners of the company.

I asked Roy at this point whether he wanted an agreement.

His reply was, "If my word isn't any good,

a stack of paper table high will not make it any better."

We built a multi-million-dollar company

with no written agreement.

Peter Pakosh and Roy Robinson
create Versatile Manufacturing Ltd. of Canada

This book is dedicated to the
loving memory of my grandparents
Peter and Adeline Pakosh.

Japonica Press

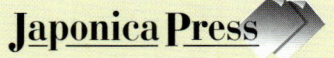

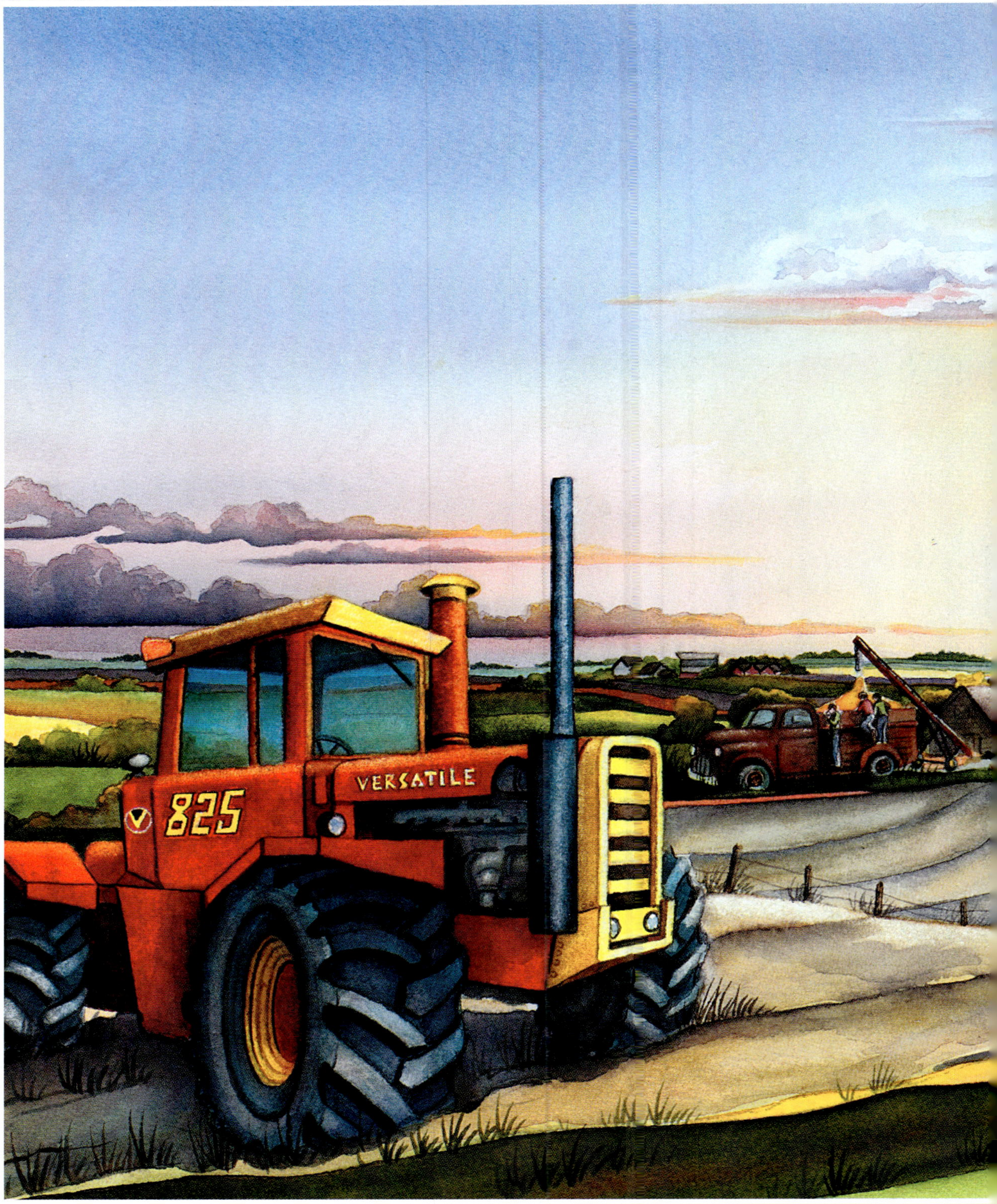

Versatile
TRACTORS

A Farm Boy's Dream

JARROD PAKOSH

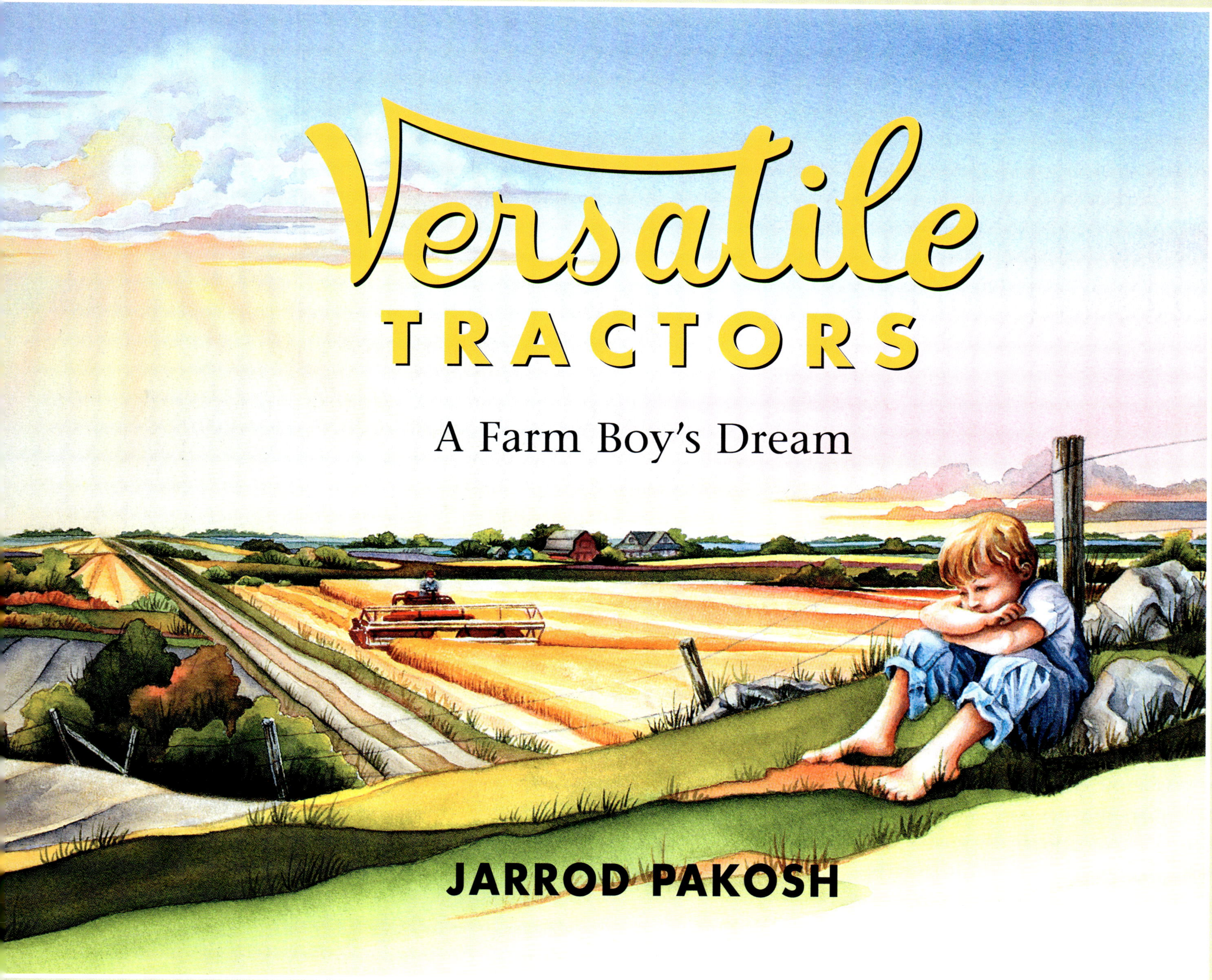

First Published 2003

Copyright © Jarrod Pakosh, 2003
The moral rights of the author have been asserted

All rights reserved. No parts of this publication may be reproduced, stored in a retrieval system, or transmitted, in any form or by any means, electronic, mechanical, photocopying, recording or otherwise, without prior permission of Japonica Press.

ISBN 1-904686-00-1

A catalogue record for this book is available from the British Library

Published by
Japonica Press
Low Green Farm, Hutton, Driffield,
East Yorkshire, YO25 9PX

United Kingdom

www.classic-tractors.co.uk

All rights reserved. All material property of the Peter Pakosh Estate. No part of this book may be reproduced or transmitted in any form or by any means without written permission from the publisher.
Visit our website at www.versatile-tractors.com

Agco, Bühler, Fiat, Ford, Hesston, John Deere, Massey Harris, New Holland, and Versatile are registered trade names.
These trade names, their trademarks, and logos may not be used without permission of their respective companies.

Title page artwork (pages 2-3) by Saskatchewan prairie artist Cyndi Tasche. All rights reserved. Website: www.cyndtasche.com
Design and layout of this book by Accu-Litho, Mississauga, Ontario, Canada.
Cover design and typesetting of this book by McCorkindale Advertising & Design, Waterloo, Ontario, Canada.

The publisher acknowledges the financial support of the Government of Canada
through the Book Publishing Industry Development Program (BPIDP), for its publishing efforts.
The publisher also gratefully acknowledges the assistance of New Holland North America,
CNH Global, Bühler Versatile Inc. and the Association of Equipment Manufacturers (AEM).

Printed in Singapore

TABLE OF CONTENTS

ACKNOWLEDGEMENTS

Thank you to my wife, Lisa, for your love, patience and support.
I would also like to thank my family, Ken and Lynn, Don and Kathy, Leah and
Aunty Rose, and my two daughters, Keana and Sydney, for all of your encouragement
and financial assistance without which this book would not have been possible.

Many thanks also to Edward Morrison, Don Wadge, Wally Sopiwnyk, Thom K. Wu,
Drayson Hendricks, Dan and Yolande Pakosh, Cameron Renton, John Denison,
Noel Hudson, Peter D. Simpson, Peter and Vickie Turner, Sean and Sandra Mitchell, John Bühler,
Karl Knisely, Stuart Gibbard and Stephen Moate and for your help and great ideas.

1

HUMBLE BEGINNINGS

A FARM BOY'S DREAM

They arrived with nothing but dreams of a better life. They journeyed with only an iron will to work, sweat and risk everything for something better. They were North America's farm immigrants.

Homesteaders found themselves dwarfed by the vast prairies. Desperate to clear raw land, they met their challenge head on, carving out wheat fields and farms from nothing, often by hand.

They simply refused to look back or give up.

You could see it in their wind-chafed faces, feel it in their dry, callused hands. They lived and worked under conditions we can't even imagine. This is the story of a farm boy's dream. A dream of making farming easier for his family and farmers everywhere. A dream that would propel him into the machinery industry and eventually secure for him a special place in history. This is the story of Peter Pakosh.

This is the story of Versatile.

My history could begin with the time my parents first came to Canada. It was 1905 when my father, Emil Pakosz, left Poland and arrived at Ellis Island. My mother, Klawda Wrona, came with her family in 1907 to Scranton, Pennsylvania, U.S.A.

My grandfather's personal memoirs appear here and in boxed excerpts throughout the book. They represent almost a century of hard work, determination and love. His words, his feelings, his dreams. I hope you find his memories as interesting and inspirational as I have.

JARROD PAKOSH

1907

That is when my father and mother met and soon they were married. They all worked hard and long hours in those days so that they could save some money to move to Canada. The government was giving any immigrant 160 acres of land for $10. This sounded very interesting to them, as in Poland they only had a few acres inherited from one generation to another. As soon as they were able to they made preparations to move to Saskatchewan.

1908

On the government-issued land, my parents built a log house plastered with a mixture of clay and straw. It was only a one-room house where they slept and ate, as it was easier to heat, as they could only use a box stove and cut wood to keep the fire going. They dug a well, built an outside toilet and started to clear the land. My Dad built a small barn and bought two oxen and a plow to start breaking the land and growing some grain.

The land was fertile and very productive. During the harvest, they were still using a scythe and binding with straw. It was okay at first, as they did not have too much land, but as they began to expand changes were inevitable.

I was born June 11, 1911. My father was very happy that it was a son.

During harvest, my mother took me out to where the sheaves were and gave me a bottle, putting me on one of the sheaves, and then started to stook. She would go home with me at about 6:00 P.M. in order to make supper for Dad. It is almost unbelievable the changes and the progress made in a technological way since then. From oxen to four-wheel-drive tractors with hydraulics to operation of the equipment like "Versatile." Little did anyone know what developments would take place in the future.

1912

The routine of clearing more land continued. Father and mother would go out to the bush with two oxen and of course they would always take me along. Dad would cut the branches around the tree and hitch the oxen pulling a chain, which Dad tied around the tree. Mother drove the oxen, pulling the tree down, with Dad cutting the remaining roots. At noon, whatever trees they had cut down they had them pulled by the oxen to the yard. The trees piled up in the yard would eventually be cut into firewood. The cutting was done by hand then split by an axe. Everything on the farm was done by hand.

1913

By 1913 their financial status began to improve, as there was an excellent demand for Canadian hard spring wheat. However, it was still beyond their financial means to get rid of the oxen and buy horses and other horse-drawn equipment. They did manage to get one horse and buggy so that they would not have to walk to Yorkton to do their shopping.

In the fall of 1913 they had a bumper crop, and grain prices skyrocketed because of the rumblings of a World War.

Centre: Early threshing gang c.1920s.
Right: Peter's father, Emil, and brother Dan working their land c.1930s.

1914

So in 1914 my Dad bought another farm, sold his homestead along with the oxen and we moved to the new place. I remember vaguely my Dad buying three more horses and a bottom plow on which a person could at least sit down while plowing. The buildings were a little shabby, but after some renovations they were habitable. At least he had a good barn, and Dad just loved his horses.

Later on he was able to purchase a seed drill and was able to put the crop more quickly and efficiently. On his original homestead all the seeding was done by hand. It was quite an improvement. My father was a very aggressive farmer still looking ahead to improve his lot in life so he could provide for the family.

1916

Mother's parents arrived in the spring of 1916 and lived with us, as we now had a two-storey house. They were of great help, as father purchased more horses and more cattle so there were a lot more chores. Hay had to be cut by scythe to feed the livestock. Raking of hay was done by hand, as we as yet did not have a rake, which could have been operated by horses. We put on a wagon and a hayrack, so my parents could load the rack and haul it home, putting it in a haystack.

In the fall of 1916 my father acquired his first binder for cutting the grain and tying it. No more scythe. That was a blessing. It was sure nice to see the sheaves come out of the binder tied with twine. I was only five years old but I already took great interest in machinery. Dad hired a steam engine outfit to do the threshing. I marvelled how it worked. The sheaves were put in the feeder. As they went through, the grain went to a box and the straw was blown into a pile behind the machine.

I stayed close by, watching how the steam engine, with a long belt, operated the threshing machine. I kept walking around looking at how all the pulleys and belts were turning. After harvest, when Dad would go plowing with four horses and a two-furrow gang plow, he let me sit on the plow, and I can still remember watching the plow turning the soil over. It just seemed so natural to mechanize the farm industry.

1918

This was a very crucial year. The Spanish flu hit the area. A few people we knew very well died. One family who were close friends of my parents, father and mother died, leaving three children as orphans. Our family were all sick but all [survived].

Centre: Peter (far right) with father, mother, sisters and a brother c.1930s.
Right: Family and friends on the farm ready to go.

1919

This proved to be a year of further expansion. My father bought a 1/4 section of land, or 160 acres. So now the family owned 1/2 section, or 320 acres, of farm land. So we moved to the house that you and Lisa saw during the Pakosh reunion gathering in 1994. My dad dismantled the old house and renovated the house that you saw and is still standing. We still used the barn and the granary across the road for a few years.

I will never forget when one of our friends from Donwell visited us with two horses and a buggy. They were already well established, as they came to the area earlier. Dad got me to unhitch the horses and take them across the road to the barn. When they were leaving I brought the horses back and hitched them to the buggy. To my surprise the man gave me 25¢ as a tip. In those days that was a lot of money. I was so happy.

My future wife, Adeline, was born on Dec. 6.

1920

In the fall of 1920 Dad was able to purchase more equipment, including putting up a couple of granaries, but best of all, one day he came home with a brand new Model T Ford.

1922

In 1922, Dad bought another farm. It also was a 1/4 section of land (160 acres). So now we had three farms. This of course meant that more farm equipment would be needed. One day

Dad brought home a brand new discer, buying it from a Donwell IHC (International Harvester dealer). I was so curious how it was made that I took it apart to see the components. My father came along, saying to me, "What the heck are you doing? This is a brand-new machine and does not need any fixing." He let me fix any equipment that needed it, as he noticed early that I was mechanically inclined. During harvest of this year I talked my older sister Julia into going with me and taking the Model T Ford for a drive. We drove for about 1/2 mile south when Dad spotted us, giving us heck and taking over.

Season by season, farm life progressed during the early '20s. In April, with spring around the corner, we would get the seed ready, as we already had our own cleaner. After seeding we would cultivate summer fallow with a cultivator and four horses. Then came the harvest, the most interesting part of the year. We still hired a threshing gang. During harvest Dad let me drive the car, taking lunches to the gang. I was so proud.

1924

In 1924 Dad bought another 1/4 section of land (160 acres) so we now had four farms. During the summers, the fields were plowed with two teams of four horses and two-gang bottom plows. Dad operated one team and mother the other. When I came home from school I would take over the team that mother used so that mother could go home to make supper.

Top: Where we were raised. Built in the 1920s.   Centre: Upstairs bedroom where all the children slept.
Bottom: Kitchen with wood stove and milk separator.

1926

Springtime came along and we would have to help with grain cleaning after school hours. Dad hired a man to help him with spring seeding, as he acquired more land and needed more help. The biggest event of my lifetime was when Dad decided to buy his own threshing outfit. After helping me to run the outfit for a few days, he says to me, "You will have to run it yourself, I have too many other things to do." I was only fifteen years old. I was a bit scared, but it wasn't long before I learned how to put belts on, line up the tractor with the machine, grease and change oil. There were no grain augers, so the grain had to be shovelled into the bins by scoop shovel.

1929

In 1929, the crunch came when a depression hit the country, not only here, but worldwide. The grain prices tumbled from $2 a bushel to 25¢ a bushel. It was a real disaster. My dad sold his out at 75¢ a bushel. Dad bought me a brand-new pair of shoes, but told me to walk barefooted until I got to school, so I wouldn't wear them out. Things were to be difficult for some time.

1930

The Depression continued. Things just came to a halt for a while; no one was buying anything, as they couldn't afford it. During the winter, I stayed in town and came home only weekends. In the spring, Dad let me take the Model T Ford to school so that I could come home after school and help with the chores. This continued until summer holidays. During the summer holidays…back on the cultivator.

The early '30s would prove to be a real challenge all across the nation and especially for the farmers.

1933

This was a crucial year for me, as I was already finished high school this year, and being the oldest son I did not know what to do. I already qualified to be a schoolteacher and go to Regina College and learn school-teaching. However I never felt like being a schoolteacher.

Dad knew that I loved mechanical things and always used me to repair the machinery, which I enjoyed very much. Besides repairing, I was starting to remodel some of the equipment. I built a snowmobile, getting parts made in local machine shops. My biggest problem was that I would get an idea but did not know how to make a working drawing, as most people who were in machine shop business worked from a design and dimensions worked out on a print. I was at a disadvantage, so I continued farming until I was sure what I wanted to do.

Top: Family barn still standing c.1930.
Centre: Peter, in living room, reminisces about farm life.
Bottom: Peter's brother-in-law Orest pitching sheaves.

1935

Well, when 1935 rolled around I declared I would drop Adeline [his girlfriend] a line. I got an immediate reply and I could see that she was thinking of me also, hoping that I could come down to Winnipeg soon.

Sometimes the way things work out almost appears as power beyond what is normal. My dad told me that maybe I should go to a trade school or something in Winnipeg and get an education, saying: "Maybe some day you will do more for your children and grandchildren than I was able to do for you." I told Dad if I went, someday I'd come home with a brand-new tractor. So in February he gave the cattle buyer $5 to take me to Winnipeg and a put few dollars in my pocket, and I was on my way to Winnipeg in a caboose. I was very happy about it, as I wanted to learn engineering and because I would see Adeline again. I enrolled in a trade school, as I wanted to be a mechanical engineer, and got myself a room nearby. At that time I could get a full-course meal for 15¢.

It wasn't long before I found out that this was what I was looking for. I had no problem getting ideas, but I did not know how to put it on paper. After a few months of school I learned drafting, or making a drawing showing top, side and front view. The professor asked me to imagine a part and put it on the paper. He then took it to a pattern maker to make it full scale out of wood. He brought it to me and asked me, "Is this what you had in mind?" I jumped with joy, as it was just what I had in mind. From then on I progressed rapidly in my designing ability and then learning stresses and strains of materials and also metallurgy and mathematics.

1936

On December 19, 1936, Adeline and I got married.

Times were still rough financially. I had to borrow $10 from a friend in order to get a marriage license. We could only give the minister a few dollars for his services. Adeline's parents made a dinner, inviting a few friends, so we had a little party. Adeline's sister, Rose, played the piano, "Here Comes the Bride," as we walked down the stairway. I will never forget embracing my wife, saying to her: "Now we are husband and wife and together we will make something out of our lives as a team." We were both young and ambitious and willing to work harder than ever to improve our lot in life. It wasn't easy, but we did it.

The next weekend we went to Mikado, Saskatchewan, by train, as my parents couldn't afford to come to the wedding. We had a few friends and a little reception congratulating us. My father and mother walked up with tears in their eyes. Dad said, "Happy landings, son," giving me a $20 bill, saying this is all we can afford. It was touching.

About a year later I got a job at a service station on Selkirk Avenue in Winnipeg, paying $15 a week. I made arrangements to keep going to school in the evening. Adeline went to work in a sewing factory, as she was very anxious for me to get the education.

Top: Peter (far left) with some in-laws.
Centre: Lunchtime during busy harvest c.1930s.
Bottom: Peter, at age 20, takes a well-deserved break.

1938

In 1938 I quit the service station and got a job as a mechanic with Black And White Taxi Company downtown. I found it very interesting because they used me as a cab driver to meet the morning trains. One time, Tommy Douglas, premiere of Saskatchewan, was my passenger. During the day I would work keeping the taxicabs in shape.

Adeline's sewing factory job was not too far away, so we rented a small apartment for a while so we could walk to work.

During the weekends we would go to Adeline's father's farm (35 miles north) near Selkirk, where Dad was trying to finish the house we started in 1935. The reason that it took so long was because it was put up with voluntary help. We did have a truck to haul materials between Winnipeg and the farm.

1939

On September 1, 1939, World War II broke out. We could hear Hitler screaming on the radio. Thousand-year reign for Germany.

Top: Caboose similar to one Peter took in 1935.
Centre: Peter ran his first threshing outfit at age 15.
Bottom: Early mechanization enthralled Peter (second from right).

1940

By 1940 I wanted to start looking for a job as a mechanical draftsman. The last call I made was at a sugar beet factory on Chevrier Boulevard in Fort Garry. Across the road from the sugar beet factory, there was a stretch of land where Versatile is now located, however at the time it never came to my mind that some day that would be the case. However, the location for some reason or other impressed me. They told me that they did not need anyone, so I decided to go home and do something else.

When I got home, I told Adeline that it's just impossible for me to get a job here, and that maybe we should head east to Toronto. Adeline was all for it and in a few days we packed all our belongings into three suitcases and took a bus via the U.S.A. to Toronto. On the way down, we decided that we would stop off at Windsor and see if I could get a job with Ford. The next day I stood in line all day for an interview, as there were many people looking for a job. At 4:00 P.M. we were told, "No more interviews today, come tomorrow." When I got to the hotel, I said, "Tomorrow? Tomorrow maybe we'd better head for Toronto," which we did.

When we arrived in Toronto I got in touch with a placement agency and told them that I was a mechanical draftsman and would like a job with Massey Harris, as I am a boy from the farm and love farm machinery. They made me an appointment with Harry Kerr and Harris Bulmer. I got a job as a draftsman for 45¢ an hour. Soon, my boss, Harry Kerr, was pleased with my accomplishments and started to give me more complicated assignments.

Peter and Adeline married in December 1936.

INVITATION

Mr. & Mrs. E. Zarysky request the honor of your presence at the marriage of their daughter Adeline to Mr. Peter Pakosh.

The wedding will take place at the bride's home, at 584 Machray Ave., Wpg. Sunday, December 20, 1936, at 11 a.m.

General reception will be held at the home of Mr. & Mrs. E. Pakosh, Mikado Sk., Sunday, December 27, 1936, at 11 a.m.

Versatile's origin and rapid growth date back to 1945 and its humble beginnings in eastern Canada. Peter Pakosh was born on June 11, 1911, and raised on a farm southwest of Mikado, Saskatchewan.

After attending four years of high school in Canora, Peter graduated in 1935 and moved to Winnipeg to attend an engineering college. Finding no work, he packed his bags and headed for Toronto.

Pakosh soon found employment as a tool designer with one of the world's largest farm-equipment manufacturers, Massey Harris. However, having been raised on a farm and been a dedicated machinery buff since early childhood, Peter grew dissatisfied with the way his career was progressing.

Left: Toronto home on Palmerston Street, where Versatile was born c.1945.
Centre: Peter and Adeline with their first son, Ken, born in 1945.
Right: Peter and Ken at work and play in the front yard.

By 1944 I was still working for Massey Harris. I loved designing and coming up with new ideas, so they gave me a promotion. They gave me a job as a chief draftsman in the mechanical department. This gave me an opportunity to roam around the plant developing new ideas for production.

He expressed a desire to be transferred into the design department, as he had some ideas about implement design. In particular, Peter was fascinated with hydraulically operated farm equipment and the potential future applications in that field. However, a head draftsman informed the assertive young designer that he would have to take a position as a tracing draftsman for some five years, along with a pay cut, before he would even be considered for a position in the design department. To Peter this was the proverbial kick in the teeth. But it did not discourage the young dreamer. Instead, it inspired him to go ahead and design equipment, "just to show them I had some good ideas."

Left: Adeline, early 1940s.
Right: Peter and Ken outside their Toronto home.

In the fall of 1944, we got the opportunity to rent a whole storey of a house on 273 Palmerston Avenue, which we did. We rented the upstairs. The basement was something else. I could see the possibility of using it for light production in a year or two. I was already thinking of a grain auger.

It was in the basement of his Toronto home that Peter's ideas took shape in metal as he began his earliest attempts to design and build his first machine. A grain auger seemed like a good project with which to start, as it was a small implement, and the budget could be met by his monthly salary from Massey. That first grain auger, without undercarriage or motor, was a success. It was a simple design with few moving parts, therefore less likelihood of failure, and it could be manufactured on a large scale quite inexpensively.

Centre: First prototype grain auger built in the backyard.
Right: Adeline and Ken playing in the yard.

The year 1946 saw me complete a prototype of an auger. In those days we were poor but happy, though as we didn't have the money we were unable to go into production. That same year I talked to Massey executives about the need for a grain auger for western farmers. They flatly rejected the idea, so on the way home that day I said to myself, "I will show them," with tears in my eyes.

Peter decided to capitalize on this small taste of success, and he purchased sufficient materials to assemble ten augers, which were sold to farmers in western Canada. These farmers accepted his first production of augers not only because they were constructed in such a simple manner, but also because they were superior to others on the market, and less expensive.

This inspired Peter to continue his design work, and in the spring of 1946 he began preparing for the construction of another fifty augers.

Top: First factory rented in Toronto for auger productions c.1946.
Botrtom left: Early drawing of first auger for advertisement purposes.
Bottom right: Factory on Eugene Street, Toronto.

I registered Hydraulic Engineering and decided to go on my own.

Fortunately, Roy Robinson came to Toronto with Rose and stayed with us. He was looking for something but did not know what. He worked at a Sudbury mine as a machinist, so he was also quite mechanically inclined. I took Roy to the backyard and showed him the auger, and also the truck.

This was when he encountered his first setback: the firm that was to supply the auger flighting refused to deliver without receiving payment in advance. Their reasoning was that Peter was not a "manufacturer," and the risk involved in one man's idea was too great. It appeared that the young designer's taste of success would be followed by the bitterness of defeat.

At this point his wife, Adeline, having complete faith in her ambitious husband, readily gave up the money she had managed to save towards her first fur coat.

Left: Peter, Adeline and Ken welcome home Don, born 1949.
Right: The Pakosh family moves to Cameron Avenue, Toronto c.1949.

I indicated to him that if he was interested we could start here and then later move to Winnipeg, as it is the centre of grain growing and where farmers are most in need of grain augers. I also told Roy that if he were interested, "whatever money I put into the company, half of it is yours."

With his wife's loving support and confidence, Peter was able to complete and sell the augers.

In the fall of 1946, another farm-raised young man entered the picture.

Roy Robinson, Peter's brother-in-law, had been born on a farm in Grand Valley, Ontario, and had begun his working career as a machinist. Now he was looking for something new. Roy decided to move to Toronto, and the pair began to exchange ideas.

Left: Roy and Rose Robinson in front of their home c.1949.
Right: Roy and Rose at their wedding in 1942.

We would each be half owners of the company. In other words, it would be a partnership.

Roy's reply was that he was interested, as he liked the idea of merchandising. I asked Roy at this point whether he wanted an agreement. His reply was, "If my word isn't any good, a stack of paper table high will not make it any better." We built a multi-million-dollar company with no written agreement.

During this period, field sprayers began entering the market. Based on their farm experience, both men realized how valuable it would prove to be for farmers; however, the price tag on these implements in the current market was, in their minds, rather high, so they boldly decided to build their own.

In late 1946, the men assembled their first field sprayer in the very basement where Peter had designed and built his grain auger just a year earlier.

First Versatile grain auger advertisement c.1940s.

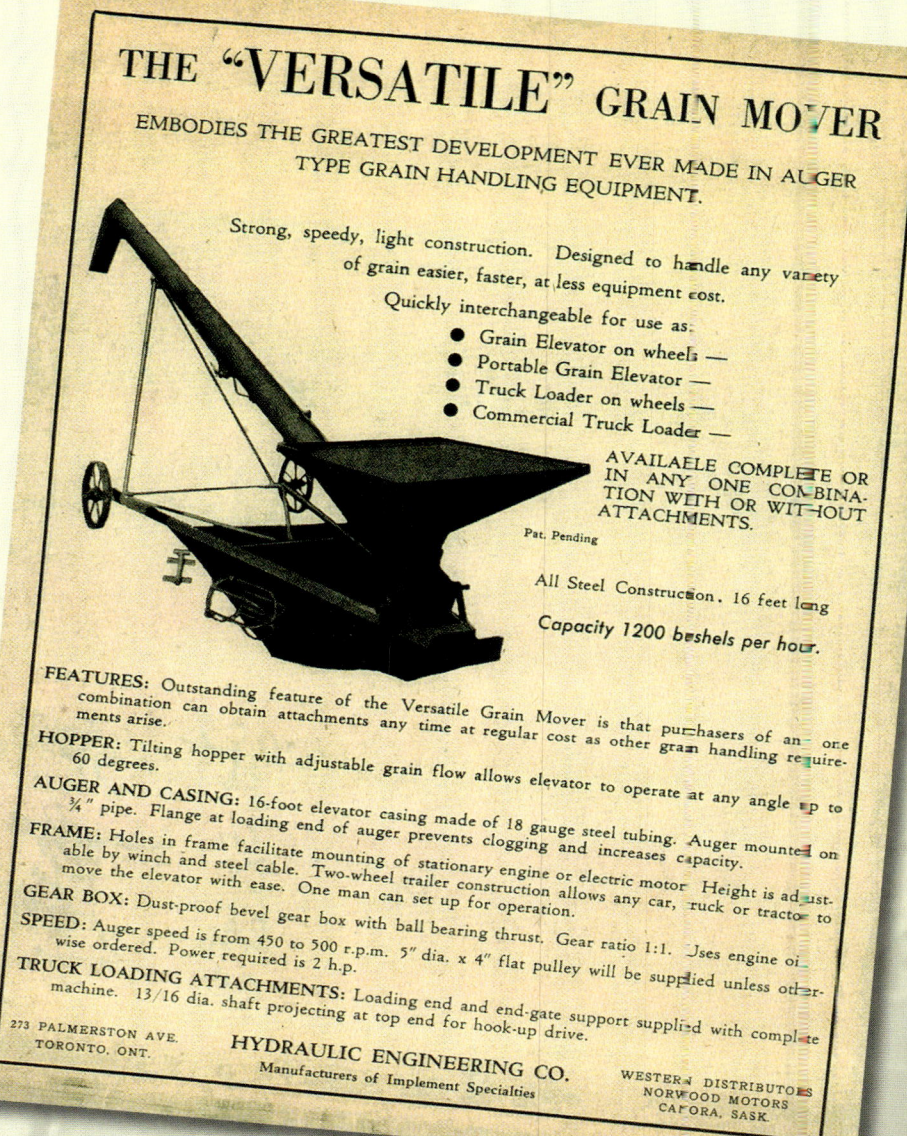

THE "VERSATILE" GRAIN MOVER

EMBODIES THE GREATEST DEVELOPMENT EVER MADE IN AUGER TYPE GRAIN HANDLING EQUIPMENT.

Strong, speedy, light construction. Designed to handle any variety of grain easier, faster, at less equipment cost.

Quickly interchangeable for use as:
- Grain Elevator on wheels —
- Portable Grain Elevator —
- Truck Loader on wheels —
- Commercial Truck Loader —

AVAILABLE COMPLETE OR IN ANY ONE COMBINATION WITH OR WITHOUT ATTACHMENTS.

Pat. Pending

All Steel Construction. 16 feet long

Capacity 1200 bushels per hour.

FEATURES: Outstanding feature of the Versatile Grain Mover is that purchasers of any one combination can obtain attachments any time at regular cost as other grain handling requirements arise.

HOPPER: Tilting hopper with adjustable grain flow allows elevator to operate at any angle up to 60 degrees.

AUGER AND CASING: 16-foot elevator casing made of 18 gauge steel tubing. Auger mounted on ¾" pipe. Flange at loading end of auger prevents clogging and increases capacity.

FRAME: Holes in frame facilitate mounting of stationary engine or electric motor. Height is adjustable by winch and steel cable. Two-wheel trailer construction allows any car, truck or tractor to move the elevator with ease. One man can set up for operation.

GEAR BOX: Dust-proof bevel gear box with ball bearing thrust. Gear ratio 1:1. Uses engine oil, wise ordered.

SPEED: Auger speed is from 450 to 500 r.p.m. 5" dia. x 4" flat pulley will be supplied unless otherwise ordered. Power required is 2 h.p.

TRUCK LOADING ATTACHMENTS: Loading end and end-gate support supplied with complete machine. 13/16 dia. shaft projecting at top end for hook-up drive.

273 PALMERSTON AVE. TORONTO, ONT.

HYDRAULIC ENGINEERING CO.
Manufacturers of Implement Specialties

WESTERN DISTRIBUTORS NORWOOD MOTORS CANORA, SASK.

Roy was the first employee. I had to keep working to bring in some money to keep operating and to feed the family. In order to get going, we rented a small shop on Brunswick and put Roy on the payroll, paying him $7 a week. I only went there evenings and weekends. I still don't know how we managed, but we did.

The men entered into a verbal partnership agreement, based only on a handshake, and decided to take their chances in the ever-growing, ever-competitive farm-implement market.

Upon completion, they realized that their sprayer, although simple in design and construction (as had been the auger), was of sound quality. Cost analysis established that mass production would be feasible and that this sprayer could very well be a strong competitor on the new market.

A model of the "fan type" sprayer which helped the company gain recognition in Western Canada during its beginnings in the late 40's.

Left: Painting Versatile sprayers by hand.
Centre: Early drawing of sprayer for advertisement purposes.
Right: Peter, his boys and Roy outside the Toronto factory c.1950s.

We started building grain augers, mostly for local consumption, to begin with. We also designed and built sprayers. Later on we started to ship them to a Winnipeg warehouse for distribution. It was tough going.

One day I said to Roy, "Maybe we should quit, as it is getting to be very hard on all of us." Roy's reply was, "Anyone can quit. That is the easiest thing to do."

With very little capital, a lot of ideas, proven designs for a grain auger and field sprayer and intense determination, a new company, the Hydraulic Engineering Company, was formed in the spring of 1947. Pakosh was in charge of design, and Robinson, due to his great administrative abilities, was in charge of purchasing, sales and manufacturing. Roy became the first employee of the newly formed company, while Peter continued his work at Massey.

Peter and Ken pose with the first Hydraulic Engineering Company truck.

So next morning we were up and at it again. Roy was tremendous in purchasing materials and being in charge of the operation. I could see his administrative ability. I started to feel that between the two of us, were I to leave Massey-Harris, we could (and did) make real headway, as neither of us were quitters.

3

BALING WIRE AND SPIT

The new company rented 2,000 square feet and swiftly began their first major production of one hundred field sprayers. Despite their having received firm orders even before the sprayers were manufactured, the supplier of the tanks refused to deliver them unless paid up front in cash. The banks, too, flatly refused to offer credit to the young entrepreneurs.

As a last resort, yet again the pair offered all of their belongings as collateral to obtain the funds necessary to continue.

Left: Sprayer parts ready for assembly c.1950.
Centre: The Pakosh family.
Right: Auger tubes in storage.

In the meantime, I still worked for M. H. and Roy ran the operation. He was good at dealing with people. I could see that before long we would have to move to a larger plant.

In 1947 we acquired the first plant that we bought in Toronto for the production of the grain augers and sprayers, though production did not start till 1948. We also bought other lots, which we sold later.

True to form, all of Hydraulic Engineering's inventory sold, and the company generated enough money not only to continue production but also to expand its product line. Thus, by the end of 1947, a third innovative product was added to the company's line of equipment, a harrow drawbar. It was then that Peter dubbed their modest line of products "Versatile."

In 1948, with the future more promising than ever, Hydraulic Engineering bought its first permanent manufacturing facility.

Left: Peter and Ken and Don.
Right: Early Versatile harrow drawbar ad.

It took us a little while to get going, but by about the middle of June the augers were in full production. They were only 17 feet long at first, and then later we also designed one that was 21 feet long.

We bought a couple of presses, welders, press drills and other small tools that we needed. Roy did all the managing, as I was still working at M. H. and worked only on evenings and weekends.

By this time, farmers from the West had begun to recognize the Versatile name and the value and quality that it stood for. By supplying quality products at lower prices, they were earning the support and loyalty of an increasing number of farmers.

I n doing so, both men risked everything and sold their farms in western Canada to finance the expansion. A staff of fifty men was hired, and greater production began as augers, sprayers and drawbars were assembled, loaded into boxcars and shipped by rail to anxious farmers across the country.

Left: First sprayer was designed to spray both left and right.
Right: This larger tank covered more acres than the competition.

The plant was only about 2,000 square feet, so we had to do a lot of work outside when it didn't rain. We also designed a sprayer for the next year's production, but in the meantime, we had to rush to ship the augers in time for western harvest.

By 1950 freight costs were climbing, seriously affecting the price of the product. It was time for a move out west.

Winnipeg, Manitoba, seemed the perfect central place to relocate. Peter was familiar with the city, and it was closer to the western market yet still close enough to the eastern steel mills.

Left: Front of 1950s harrow drawbar pamphlet.
Right: Back of same.

During the winter of 1948, we were still operating from the Brunswick plant, but towards spring we had our first opportunity to buy our own plant.

By the fall we were in full production, shipping augers to Winnipeg for distribution. It wasn't the best arrangement, but it was the best we could do.

eter's first and foremost desire was to develop a self-propelled implement driven by hydrostatic oil pressure —he had long dreamed of the possibilities. Hydraulic drives were quite scarce during those years due to a lack of mass production in this field. Units were also very expensive and mainly confined to industrial uses. Peter produced 100 such units before temporarily postponing production in favour of his first mechanically driven self-propelled swather.

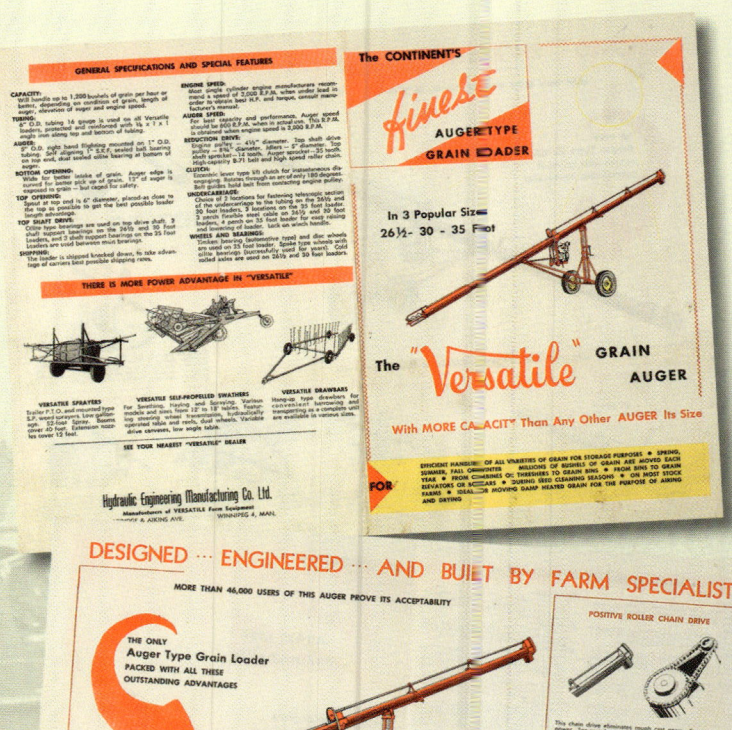

Above: The Versatile model 103 self-propelled swather.
Top right: Early auger and complete line advertisement.
Bottom right: Designed, engineered and built by farm specialists.

They put up a new plant with a conveyor and, as the combine moved along slowly, parts were put on it at different stations.

This was the year they organized the harvest brigade and shipped hundreds of combines starting  *in Texas and working north to Canada. They had pictures of ten combines working on one large field. They gave everyone a harvest brigade badge. I still have mine pinned on my EMI award.*

were made to outlast the competitors' products but still bear a price tag to suit those hard-working men in the fields. Pakosh and Robinson were ready to take on the farm equipment giants!

Peter Pakosh doing what he loved c.1955.

He believed that his equipment should be designed so that it was cost efficient and easy to repair, and able, if necessary, to be repaired in the field "using baling wire and spit." Always thinking of the farmer first, his designs

Now that we were living on Cameron Avenue I still drove to M. H., which was a long way, and Roy drove to Eugene Street with the first brand-new company car. He was sure happy with it. He did real well operating the plant. He would call me at M. H. almost every day on certain problems that came up. I would help after hours and on Saturday.

In the spring of 1951 I decided to leave and gave my notice. When my boss found out about it, he really wasn't surprised, as I had talked to him before about quitting.

By 1954 the first Versatile self-propelled swathers were on the market. A new foreman, Bill Richter, was hired to oversee production. Bill and Peter worked so well together that it was often said that each knew what the other was thinking. The Model 103 swathers used Wisconsin air-cooled engines and had variable reel speeds for different crops and conditions, but most importantly, they were the only ones that had a conventional steering wheel. The competition's swathers still had awkward, lever-actuated clutch-drive systems and just too many moving parts. Peter's first attempt at designing a self-propelled machine would eventually prove him to be a true innovator.

The 103 swather — Versatile's most popular mechanically driven SP swather — and the last model of its kind before the hydrostatic.

Top: Nature's bounty.
Bottom left: The mechanically driven model 103.
Bottom right: Model 103 with sprayer attachment.

He knew that I already had something started with Roy and said to me, "I want to give you a bit of advice. When you go on your own, never copy anybody's design. If you do, the other fellow will find his mistakes first and will be ahead of you. Be original in your designing and let other people copy you. You will find your mistakes first and will always be ahead of the other fellow. I wish you well. If you need advice don't be afraid to call me or come to my home."

4

DAVID VERSUS GOLIATH

As history had proven before, however, nothing would come easy. A drastic economic downturn developed in Canada and again threatened the company's existence. Wasting no time, Roy began investigating potential markets in the northern United States, and found dealers in North Dakota and Montana who would buy their augers and swathers almost as fast as they rolled off the assembly line.

Left: Peter Pakosh
Top right: Versatile loader advertisement.
Bottom right: Artist rendition of swather.

When I joined the company full-time, I started immediately on increasing production, as Roy had done the groundwork. We hired more people, and were still shipping sprayers and grain augers by rail and distributing them from Winnipeg. However, Roy got hold of a few dealers to whom we were shipping direct. The name of the company was still Hydraulic Engineering Co., but the product was labelled "Versatile."

These timely sales kept the firm afloat, and their swather design began to be recognized as a viable alternative in the self-propelled swather market. It took time, but by 1956 the market had opened up for the Versatile swather in the two states, as well as in Canada. That year, Wally Sopiwnyk was hired on as Roy's personal assistant, a man whom during his three decades at Versatile would prove invaluable to the growth of the company.

By 1957 South Dakota and Minnesota were added to the company's list of sales territories.

Left: Versatile swather advertisement.
Centre: 55-, 61- and 67-foot augers.
Right: Roy Robinson

It was during the summer that we started to wonder if it would not be better to move the company to Winnipeg, as the equipment we were building was all for western Canada and the central U.S.

Winnipeg would be an ideal place to manufacture machinery.

By now, the introduction of the 103 swather had been a rude awakening to the larger competitors. Versatile could no longer be ignored. Their new self-propelled swather was superior in design and carried a far more reasonable price tag. There was a clear appeal to the average farmer's budget.

Left: Swather frame under production c.1959.
Right: Early welding was all done by hand.

For instance, shipping Briggs and Stratton engines for grain augers to Toronto from Milwaukee was the same cost as shipping them from Milwaukee to Winnipeg.

So we could see a definite advantage to moving.

In September, I volunteered to drive to Winnipeg to look for property. We found 2 acres at Partridge and Aikens, and after talking to Roy, we bought it and started to build.

Some worried competitors, who had been selling their equipment for some one hundred years, began threatening their own dealers with cancellation of contracts if a single Versatile swather was found on their sales lot. It was shaping up to be the classic David-versus-Goliath conflict!

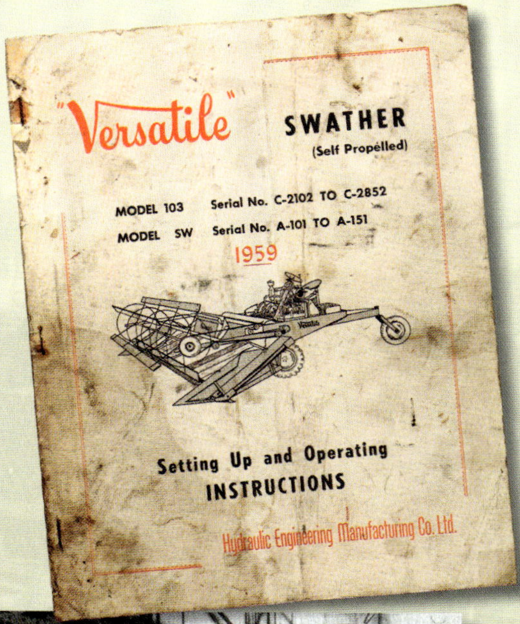

"Versatile" SWATHER
(Self Propelled)

MODEL 103   Serial No. C-2102 TO C-2852
MODEL SW   Serial No. A-101 TO A-151
1959

Setting Up and Operating
INSTRUCTIONS

Hydraulic Engineering Manufacturing Co. Ltd.

Left: Peter addresses dealers and distributors c.1959.
Top right: 1959 model 103 manual.
Bottom right: Famous Versatile red paint being applied in the paint shop.

I left Winnipeg in early October and left Roy Zarysky in charge of construction. The construction continued, and by the end of March most of the machinery for production was in place.

Roy Robinson moved down in February, while I still stayed back to ship the rest of the equipment from the 49 Eugene Street plant.

This time, though, the boys were ready for battle. By now, Peter and Roy had learned enough about the market to stay one step ahead. Rather than be intimidated, they flooded the market before the competitors could carry out the threats.

This left the competitors in the position that, should they carry out their threats, they would have to cancel almost all of their contracts, leaving a wide-open market in their own sales territories. Versatile was poised and ready.

The success of the 103 would lead to the next generation of Versatile swathers.

It took hard work to reorganize the production equipment, as we were tooling up for high production of grain augers for next year and also developing new farm equipment. New sprayers and self-propelled swathers were already on the board.

During the winter of 1953, Roy decided to try and open up the market in the central U.S. He was surprised at the interest, but we had a good grain auger at a low price.

The M-10 pull-type swather, an addition to the Versatile line of quality implements in 1960 and still a popular item on farms today.

By 1960 the market had readily accepted Versatile products, and the company was on the move and one to be watched. Also during that year, a pull-type swather was added to Versatile's line of quality farm equipment, with 250 machines produced. The M-10 pull-type, centre-delivery swather, proved to be a valuable addition. It became a popular item on many farms.

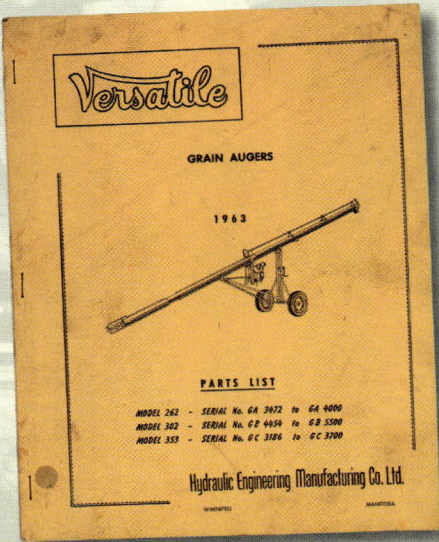

Top left: M-10 pull-type swather which expanded the company's line.
Bottom left: Fort Garry assembly line c.mid-1960s.
Centre: 1963 auger parts list.
Right: M-10 centre-delivery pull-type swather advertisement.

The orders just kept pouring in. We hired a few high-powered salesmen, and by spring, with Roy's optimism, we decided to build 2,000 grain augers.

Of course to do it we needed a large bank loan. The bank manager from CIBC [Canadian Imperial Bank of Commerce], Main and Dufferin, where we were dealing, came over and asked how much money we needed. I'll never forget him looking at Roy and saying, "That's more than the place is worth."

Over the next few years, Hydraulic Engineering Company and the Versatile line of equipment would literally begin to change the western landscape, painting it red and yellow. After years of struggle and countless setbacks, Peter and Roy finally tasted success, as Versatile began growing beyond their wildest dreams.

Outlook and Opinion

1. The Management of the Company has demonstrated its ability to expand sales and manufacturing facilities in a competitive industry.

2. The one risk this Company or any other Company doing business in the grain-growing areas of the continent cannot protect itself against is the risk of crop failures. Versatile, because of its debt-free capitalization, and its ability to contract overhead quickly can protect itself against disastrous effects of general crop failures throughout its entire market area.

3. Cash farm incomes are rising in Western Canada and the United States. Farm equipment sales outlook for Western Canada and United States is brighter today than at any time since the immediate post-war period.

SCHEDULE "A"

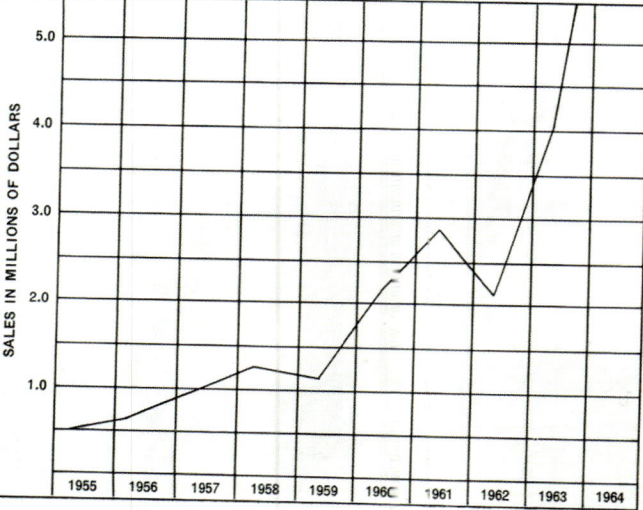

Left: Early Versatile investment prospectus c.1963.
Centre: Big prairie sky.
Right: Sales chart shows Versatile's early growth.

He went to the plant, looked around, and in about half an hour was back and said to Roy and myself, "You are a couple of young, ambitious fellows. I'll take a chance on you." So we got the money and sold all 2,000 grain augers that year.

In 1954 I designed our first self-propelled swather, Model 103, and decided to build initial production for all delivery.

5

VERSATILE MANUFACTURING LIMITED

In 1963 the firm was officially incorporated as a public company under the name Versatile Manufacturing Ltd. It was listed shortly thereafter on the Toronto Stock Exchange. By the end of the year the company had sold, in an area including five provinces and eleven states, a total of 1,049 sprayers, 1,492 grain loaders and 3,633 swathers.

Left: The Chairman of the Board.
Top right: Versatile's first stock certificate c.1964.
Bottom right: The Fort Garry plant from the sky.

The production of grain augers and sprayers was already going well, so we thought we would go to another product, as by now we had over 200 dealers in Canada and the central U.S.A., and 100 employees.

Growing rapidly, the company decided to build a new head office and factory building in the Winnipeg suburb of Fort Garry. The new 168,000-square-foot plant soon became the largest swather production facility in the world, rolling out 5,000 units in 1964 alone. Versatile's swathers now accounted for 60 percent of the sales of these machines in North America.

Top: Architect's rendition of Fort Garry plant.
Bottom left: First SP420 self-propelled combine.
Bottom right: Versatile became the largest swather maker in the world.

In the fall of the year, our dealer at Piapot, Saskatchewan, had a problem with one of our swathers. He insisted that someone come immediately, as the farmer wanted to return it. We hired a pilot to fly us out, as I didn't have my license yet. We fixed the swather and went to where the plane was. It was gone. The pilot had flown back to Winnipeg alone. We phoned Adeline and Rose to drive by car to pick us up at Moose Jaw.

Selling high-capacity machines at a lower price than the competitors was the key to their success. In the meantime, the larger farm-machinery companies would sell their equipment to their branches, and the branches would sell to the dealers. By the time it got to the farmer, the price tag would have risen by as much as 50 percent. Versatile, though, had no branches, only dealers, so they were able to pass on substantial savings to the farmer.

Specialization has been key to success of Versatile Mfg.

One of the biggest farm machine firms failed to see talent in its own ranks. Result: booming new firm, competition

By J. K. EDMONDS

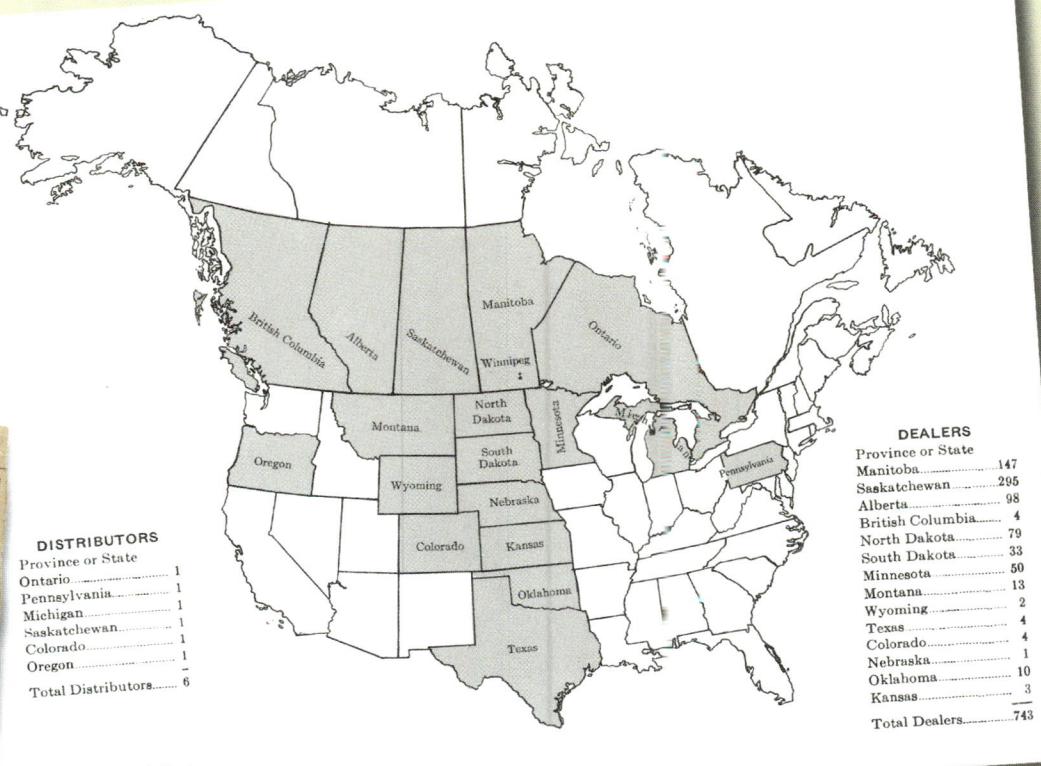

DISTRIBUTORS

Province or State	
Ontario	1
Pennsylvania	1
Michigan	1
Saskatchewan	1
Colorado	1
Oregon	1
Total Distributors	6

DEALERS

Province or State	
Manitoba	147
Saskatchewan	295
Alberta	98
British Columbia	4
North Dakota	79
South Dakota	33
Minnesota	50
Montana	13
Wyoming	2
Texas	4
Colorado	1
Nebraska	4
Oklahoma	10
Kansas	3
Total Dealers	743

‡ Head Office and Plant

Left: *The Winnipeg Tribune*, July 4th, 1964.
Right: Distributors and dealers throughout North America.

During 1955 production was normal. Sales were real good. We now had four products: grain augers, sprayers, harrow drawbars and self-propelled swathers. One day at the end of September, Roy decided that we should go selling by plane, writing up next year's orders.

The larger plant also allowed for further growth in Versatile's product line. Shortly after its official opening, the PT42 pull-type combine was introduced. It was the first combine ever made in western Canada and posed a large threat to national farm-machinery companies, which had confined their production plants to the East.

VERSATILE MANUFACTURING LTD.
first annual report: nineteen sixty four

Top left: Fort Garry combine production in full swing.
Top right: 1964 Annual Report.
Bottom: The harvest is great.

We flew to Calgary; Medicine Hat; Moose Jaw; Yorkton; Billings, Montana; and a couple of other places. Past Neepawa we flew through cloud and almost got into a tailspin. It was scary. When we came through the cloud and could see the ground about 1,000 feet below, we levelled off and flew the rest of the way to Winnipeg at that elevation.

Rides to success on philosophy

Roy Robinson, manager and original partner of Hydraulic Engineering and Manufacturing Company Ltd., Winnipeg, rode to success in the farm machinery business on one philosophy — quality and low cost.

The story of the company is the story of Mr. Robinson, who is just tying up the ends of a new plant in Fort Garry (Man.) where the Famous Versatile trade name will appear for the first time on a combine. Production will probably be in full stride this month. The same firm has been reorganized under the name of Versatile Manufacturing Ltd., retaining the same management personnel.

In a highly competitive business, he has kept his company healthy by putting in 16-hour days, seven days a week. Factory direction is only part of his job. Through personal drive he has captured a major share of the swather business in Canada, and 40 per cent of production has gone to the United States.

Mr. Robinson expects his combine sales across the border will be about the same percentage as the swather.

In the 10 years since the first Versatile swather was turned out, the plant's entire production has been sold. Now solidly based in the manufacture and sales of swathers, grain loaders, sprayers, Mr. Robinson is confidently breaking new ground in combines.

Since 1954, 11,350 swathers with the Versatile trade mark, have moved onto farms with the 1962 figure of 2,000.

In a business field where reorganization and refinancing has been a regular factor, Hydraulic Engineering has maintained a constant steadiness in production and ...

The new four-and-a-half acre factory will start production with little fanfare — Mr. Robinson does not believe in it. But his endeavors will be carrying the new combines across the prairies this summer with the same impact that drew a farmer's remark at a demonstration in Lucky Lake, Sask. last year.

"If there were a few more men like this in our country, Canada wouldn't belong to the United States."

— ROBINSON

— PAKOSH

The Versatile new combine

The D100 had 100 hp at the drawbar and carried a 363-ci, 6-cylinder Ford diesel engine. Its cousin, the G100, had a 318-ci, 8-cylinder Chrysler gas engine. Transmissions were three speeds forward and one reverse, coupled to a four-range transfer case. This gave the tractors twelve forward speeds and four reverse.

Early Production

Top left: *Winnipeg Free Press*, February 5, 1964.
Bottom left: Restored G100 on an American farm.
Right: Early tractor production c.1967.

Right after the fire, we started to make arrangements to rebuild the plant. The refurbishing program took till spring of the year. We already had a lot of orders for augers, sprayers and swathers for delivery during this year. Fortunately, by May we were back in operation and were able to meet the production orders that we had on hand.

These first articulated models were not fancy and had no cab option, but sold for less than $10,000. Ease of operation, along with the price, immediately attracted farmers to these well-built machines, and over one hundred units were sold in 1966.

4 WHEEL DRIVE TRACTOR

Versatile

MANUFACTURING LTD.

Top left: D100 currently in restoration in Manitoba.
Bottom left: Workers busy on the line c.1967.
Right: 1966 Annual Report insert.

In 1957 Steve Hrab joined the company as a combine designer. I knew him from M. H. and so we started to design combines. The following year was a combine year. It took a little while to design it and test it before we went into production; however, by fall of the year we had a model for testing.

That same year, Versatile's first SP420 self-propelled combine came off the assembly line. It had Versatile's unique straight-through design and increased body height to give extra straw-walker clearance. It also boasted a powerful, 318-cubic-inch Chrysler V8 industrial motor. The SP420 became another popular item on farms.

Top left: Executives pick a strange place for a meeting.
Bottom left: SP420 combine specifications.
Right: Golden harvest viewed from a Versatile.

In the meantime the facilities were upgraded, including manufacturing equipment, so that we could increase grain loaders, as the orders were just pouring in. By now we had over 300 dealers, so in early spring we decided to go all out on grain auger production. Going to the bank first, the same manager told us, after looking at the financial statement, that we were doing so well that he would authorize the bank to loan us all the money we needed.

The D100 and G100 were followed, in 1967, by the D118, the G125 and the D145. With the D100 still available, Versatile now offered a greater choice of models that included one with a gas engine and three with diesel engines. The D118 was equipped with a 352-ci Cummins V6 diesel engine that produced 118 drawbar horsepower.

Left: Tractor specification advertisement c.1967.
Top right: Combines ready for delivery.
Bottom right: The 1967 4WD tractor line.

After a meeting with our ten salesmen, covering Manitoba, Saskatchewan and Alberta and the central U.S., (plus, of course, the main one, Roy Robinson himself), we decided to buy materials for 4,000 grain augers. Many times Roy and Rose would be on the road at 4:00 A.M. in order to get to the farthest dealer and work back. We sold all the augers and this really put the company on solid financial footing.

The G125 had a heavy-duty 391-ci Ford V8 gasoline-driven engine. This tractor tested at over 125 drawbar horsepower and was the most affordable model, selling for $8,600.

Left: Promoting Versatile's quality and price.
Top right: Gas engine, 125-hp G125 c.1967.
Bottom right: Freshly painted and labelled G125.

In 1959 we got organized for combine production. We bought a brand-new hydraulic press that could bend metal 12 feet long, as there were a lot of special-sized angles on the combine. Because of combine production we had to cut back on auger production, however we were still able to make quite a few, including sprayers and new, improved, self-propelled swathers.

Later that year, an upgraded 470-ci Cummins V8 diesel engine model, the D145, was introduced. Its powerful, hard-working diesel engine produced 145 drawbar horsepower. The most expensive model at the time, the D145 sold for $12,200.

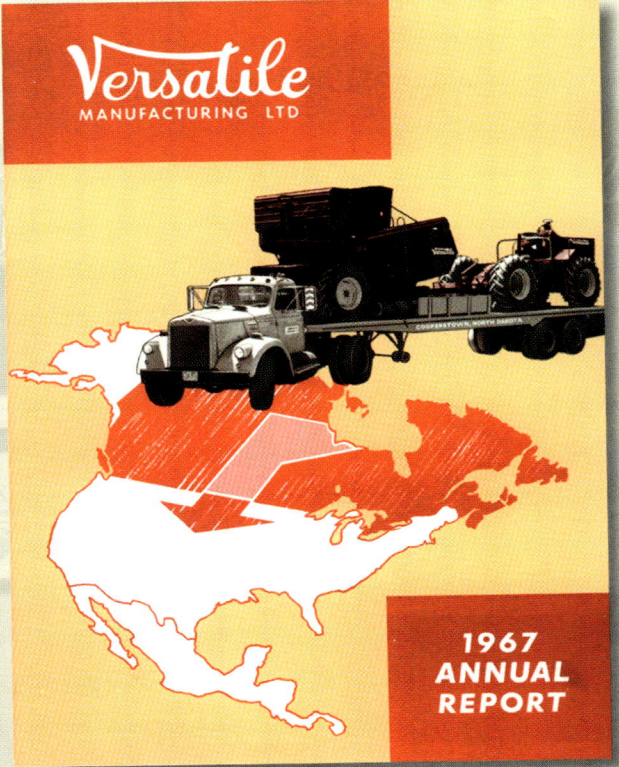

Top left: Quality control being implemented.
Bottom left: 1967 model D118.
Right: 1967 Annual Report.

During the summer we all got busy to make sure that we got all the production ready for shipping by fall. We already had close to 200 workers. Everyone contributed. One day one of the suppliers walked in and asked Roy, "How many people do you have working for you?" Roy said, "I hope all of them."

Versatile Manufacturing Ltd. Bucking Farm Machine Trend

By BRUCE McDONALD
Editor, Free Press Weekly

These new models had heavy-duty transmissions with a wide range of speeds, and easy, one-hand, centre-pivot hydrostatic steering. With working speeds of 3.1, 3.7, 4.2, 4.8, 5.4 and 6.3 mph, the operator had a greater choice in selecting the most effective speed for each individual job. The models would later all become available with custom cabs.

Left: *Winnipeg Free Press*, August 10, 1968.
Top right: "You're ahead when you buy a Versatile."
Bottom right: Fresh off the line, a new G125.

The sales went very well. Roy made his usual trip to the U.S., booking orders for next year in the late fall.

The beginning of the year was still tough on me, as I still had to look after a lot of details. It wasn't until about the middle of the year that I really started to see daylight and was back on the board. Prototype combines worked well enough, but improvements had to be made.

Though not actually first on the market, Versatile was the first to mass-produce four-wheel-drive tractors. The larger competitors had attempted this earlier but were unsuccessful because high production costs had placed their tractors in a price range far out of reach of even the largest farmers.

Left: Versatile's largest model in the sixties, the D145.
Centre: Four-wheel-drive advertisement c.1967.
Right: The *Financial Post*, February 4, 1967.

We decided to make provisions for our own tool room, purchasing the necessary equipment, and hired six tool makers so that we could tool up for our own parts for our various products. It worked so well that we thought it was time to handle another product. Besides the self-propelled swather, there was a need for a pull-type swather, so I decided to work on it myself, as Steve was very busy tooling up and improving components on the combines.

Versatile could boast of their tractors being constructed of true Versatile-designed components such as heavy-duty axles and transmissions. This allowed a price tag even some of the smaller farmers could afford. In fact, the price was equal to that of the competitors' smaller two-wheel-drive tractors.

Top left: D145 outside Fort Garry plant c.1967.
Bottom left: A Versatile cultivator.
Right: M-103 double swath swather ad.

With united effort we designed a pull-type swather powered by tractor PTO. In the fall of 1961 we shipped it to Julian Derkatch for testing. Julian sure liked it. He said it worked like a sewing machine.

We now had three models of combines: self-propelled, pull-type powered by tractor power take-off, and also a pull-type powered by its own engine. This was the year New Holland first wanted to buy us out.

S implicity of design was also key. Other tractors had to be hauled to dealers' service shops for repair, taking days, while Versatile's design allowed for modules to be replaced in the field, in hours. Farmers loved it!

Top left: A Versatile pull-type swather.
Bottom left: A G125 in plant from behind.
Right: Accessories truly made the products "Versatile."

The year 1962 was a normal one for planning and purchasing parts for production. We now had three models of combines and two models of swathers, besides improved grain augers and the drawbars. It took a lot of work and correspondence getting quotations and then ordering. Roy had the front office with a private secretary. There were three girls looking after the paperwork in the main office, preparing and doing the mailing. Steve and myself handled the designing next to the main office.

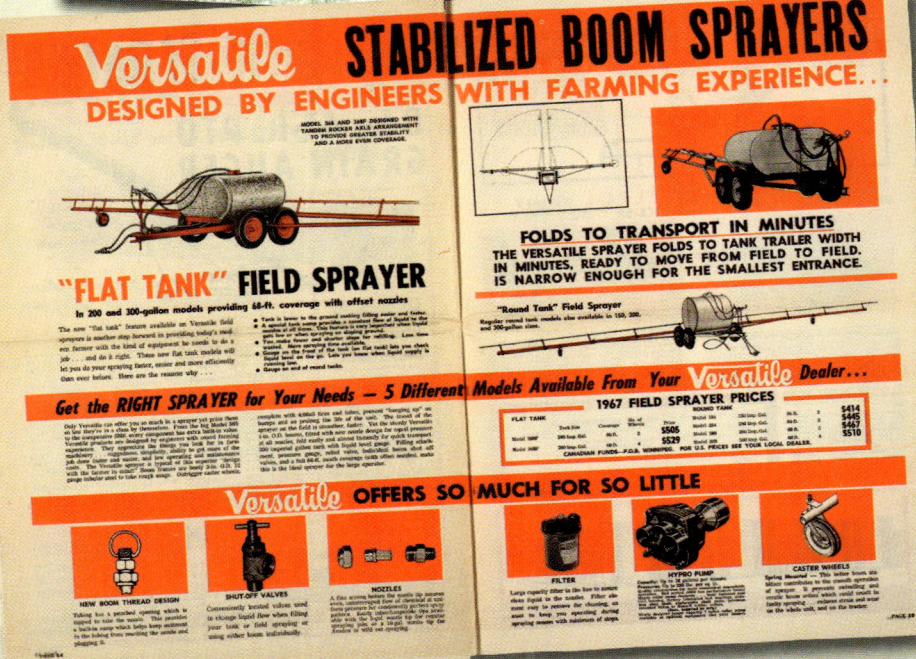

Versatile marketed their tractors as having three distinct advantages over the conventional two-wheel-drive tractor:

1. Speed—Because of the extra pulling power on four wheels, farmers could plow, cultivate and seed a greater area in less time.

2. Efficiency—Because of the flotation on four wheels, farmers could work their land sooner, even on wet ground.

3. Economy—Because of experienced manufacturing efficiency, Versatile could price their four-wheel-drive tractors for less than two-wheel types of equal power class.

Top left: The D145 (with cab) had 145 drawbar horsepower.
Bottom left: The Versatile boom sprayer was designed to fold in minutes.
Right: Peter and Roy inspect their creation.

The operation was getting quite big and was starting to get crowded. We felt that maybe we better start looking for land to build a new factory. We found acreage, which is now 1260 Clarence Avenue in Winnipeg, and decided to purchase it, as it was a good location to ship south and west. So we bought 37 acres. This was to be our biggest project of all time.

In 1963 I started to lay out the main plant area. There

Only a year after entering the market, Versatile had advance orders for all of the tractors coming off its line. Once again, the company needed to expand, and in March 1967 opening ceremonies were held for a 127,200-square-foot addition to the Fort Garry factory.

Left: Experimental hydrostatic unit checks out!
Top right: D118 introduced at plant expansion c.1967.
Bottom right: 1968 D118, G125 and D145 parts book.

was a house on the property, which we used for a temporary office. I was out there almost every day with the construction crew laying out the ground for foundation and making sure that it was located properly so that we could make the best use of the land later. The foundation was laid in the spring of the year. Versatile was born.

We had limited production in 1964, as everything was new to everybody.

By now, the SP420 combine had also gained wide acceptance and paved the way for the next generation of farm implements, an innovation Pakosh had dreamed of for over twenty years.

Top left: D118 sitting proud under the prairie sunshine.
Bottom left: 1968 Annual Report.
Right: Versatile's growth illustrated.

However, we made sure that the swather line was set up first, as it was our bread-and-butter product. We set up a conveyor line so that the swathers would move from station to station, parts put on it as it moved along. This was the Model 103 self-propelled swather. There was a tremendous market in the U.S., as in Texas they start cutting in May. So we really put the pressure on in order to meet the demand.

6

A FARM BOY'S DREAM

The farming community anxiously received Versatile's newest innovation, the Versatile self-propelled swather with hydrostatic drive, in 1968. This was the culmination of the farm boy's twenty-year-old dream, as mass production of hydraulic drives now made them affordable.

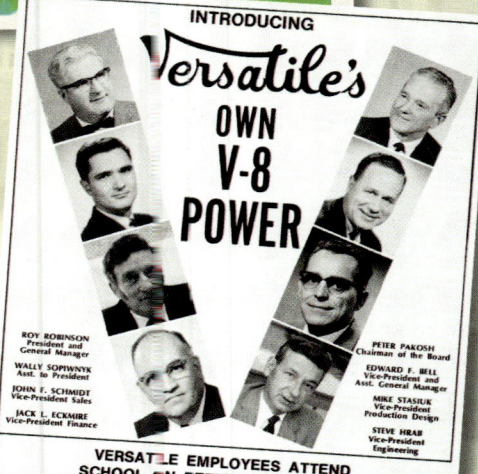

Left: 1969 Annual Report (front).
Top right: 1969 Annual Report (back).
Bottom right: Versatile's winning team of executives.

We also concentrated on combine production, as some farmers combined without swathing first. However, North and South Dakota, Minnesota and Montana always swathed first and then would start combining. With the production rolling, it gave time to start laying out the front offices. They made a few changes but not by much. It took time to lay it out and start construction.

A few companies already had hydraulically driven swathers on the market, but the SP400 was miles ahead of the competition in both design and price. The famous Model 400 hydrostatic-drive swather became widely used in hay and grain swathing applications throughout North America.

Left: Prototype skidder tractor for lumber industry circa early 1970s.
Top right: The Versatile skidder tractor never went into production.
Bottom right: Versatile's first SP400 Hydrostatic swather c.1968.

The new self-propelled swather, Model 400, was introduced in 1965, while the Model 103 self-propelled swather was deleted. During the summer of this year things were going quite smoothly as far as production was concerned; however,

because of the increase in sales, we started to put on another addition the same size as the original. The office staff was still working from the house.

In 1970 Peter's method of hydrostatic drive was carried further with the introduction of a new self-propelled combine, the SP5000, with full hydrostatic drive. This model boasted another first in the combine market—it contained a double set of straw-walkers, which ensured better separation of the grain kernels from the straw and chaff with less loss over the end of the walkers.

5000

Versatile

Top left: SP5000 combine offloading grain into hopper.
Bottom left: Peter enjoyed harvest-time late into his life.
Right: SP5000 combine brochure c.1970.

Roy's theory was that production comes first, that is how we make our money. The office is just an overhead. However, after the addition was up, we started to finish the

front offices plus the second storey where all the engineering staff and draftsmen were located.

In the early 1970s, Versatile began to release its next generation of four-wheel-drive tractors with the 700, 800, 850 and 900 Series. These new models were the first with Versatile's newly designed look and logo. The first released was the Model 700, in 1972, which arrived to huge fanfare. A parade of dealers and customers flocked to Winnipeg to view the prototype and production models.

There was so much enthusiasm that retail sales orders were received for half of the scheduled production before the assembly line even began.

Top left: Model 700 4WD at work c.1972.
Bottom left: Brochure expounding the 700's features.
Right: Safety first in 700 rollover test c.1971.

In the fall of this year we thought we'd handle another product. It was the Model 100 four-wheel-drive tractor. I'd been fascinated by the possibility of producing an inexpensive four-wheel-drive tractor for several years, and we'd kicked around its potential. The trick would be to design one that wouldn't be a luxury. To mass produce such a machine was a radical move.

1973 ANNUAL REPORT

VERSATILE

The Versatile 700 had a 555-ci Cummins V8 diesel with 220 hp at 2,850 rpm. Versatile was the first to have an officially registered roll-over protection cab, with their model 700. Another Versatile innovation was the "Murphy" safety switch, which allowed the engine to automatically shut off when oil pressure became too low or coolant temperatures too high.

Left: 1973 line-up included the 700, 800 850 and 900 models.
Top right: 1973 Annual Report.
Bottom right: Model 800 outside the factory c 1973.

The majors were saying that four-wheel drives were unwarranted, but what they were really saying was that they were timid. Their decision makers were unwilling to take risks. Innovation was restricted by their ponderous system of justification.

Versatile had indeed achieved something very special and important in the industry—confidence—which was not misplaced. Only a few Model 700 tractors remained unsold by year end.

The 800 model had a 250-hp Cummins N-855 V6 diesel engine. The Cummins NT-855 turbocharged Model 850 was rated at 280 hp.

Top left: SP400 hydrostatic swather in action.
Bottom left: SP400 manual circa mid-1970s.
Right: New 400 on display.

We received a University of Manitoba report stating the superiority and fuel efficiency of four-wheel drives and that did it. We jumped into mass-production, the first company to move. It was 1966 and we were able to price them at the same cost as the competition's conventional tractors. Still, we were sticking our necks out again.

Next came the 900 model, which was the largest in the field at the time. Referred to as "the Grandaddy of Them All," it had a Cummins V-903 V8 diesel and was rated at 300 hp. All four Versatile models had a maximum operating weight of 28,000 pounds.

Versatile was now the leader in the four-wheel-drive market.

Left: 1973 operation manual for models 800 and 850.
Centre: Model 800 with 12 bottoms.
Right: Model 900's ready to roll.

By late summer 1966, we built one hundred of the Model 100 four-wheel-drive tractors. They were all shipped to dealers so they could resell them to farmers for their fall work. They worked well, but most of the farmers were starting to look for higher-powered tractors, so we designed a new one, the Model 145 four-wheel-drive tractor. It had no cab from the beginning, but because of demand we went into production.

The Model 300 "hydro-mech" row-crop tractor was next to be released in 1973. This was Versatile's first model with "live" power takeoff and was notable because of its ability to be driven both hydrostatically and mechanically. Steve Hrab was heavily involved in this project.

Left: Hydro-mechanical model 300 in potatoes.
Centre: The 700 with 80-foot drawbar.
Right: At the controls of a Versatile 800.

By 1967 the American market for the Model 145 tractor really opened up. We could hardly keep up with the sales. It was of our own design.

I designed the transmission, housing and the different assembly; however, all the gears were provided by a Japanese company, except the final wheel-reduction gears, which were purchased in the U.S.

Peter's innovative mind and love for designing was as evident as ever. He had a drafting board in his bedroom at home and spent many sleepless nights recording his ideas on paper. At Versatile, his passion was even more evident.

Once, when trying to convey an idea to the design department, Peter got down on his knees in his suit, and with a piece of chalk, drew his schematic right there on the factory floor. The chairman of the board always remained just a farm boy at heart!

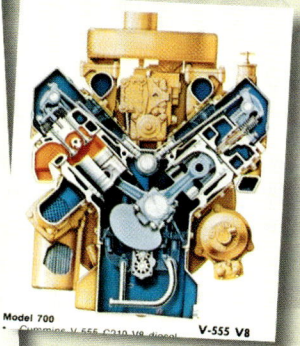

SERIES 2
Today's Investment for the Future

Top left: Features of Cummins engines explained.
Bottom left: Close-up of the Cummins V-555 engine.
Right: Series 2 introduction manual c.1975.

The year 1968 proved to be the biggest one yet in our expansion. Because we were anticipating a much greater increase in tractor, combine and swather sales, we felt that we had no choice but to expand the plant. We hired a local contractor, and by mid-summer we had a total of 11 acres of manufacturing facilities under our roof. We had to hire more employees, and by now we had 400 production workers. We had to, of course, reorganize production lines for all the products.

Soon afterward came the Series 2 Versatiles. The models included the 700, 750, 800, 825, 850, 900 and 950. The 700 had a 210-hp Cummins V-555 V8 diesel. The 750 was equipped with a 220-hp Cummins N-855 in-line 6-cylinder engine.

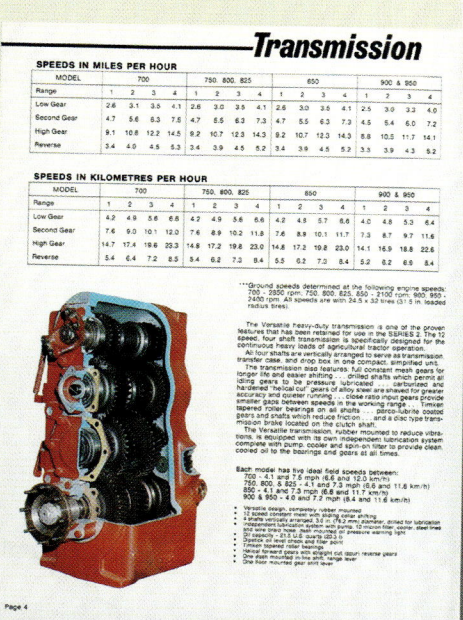

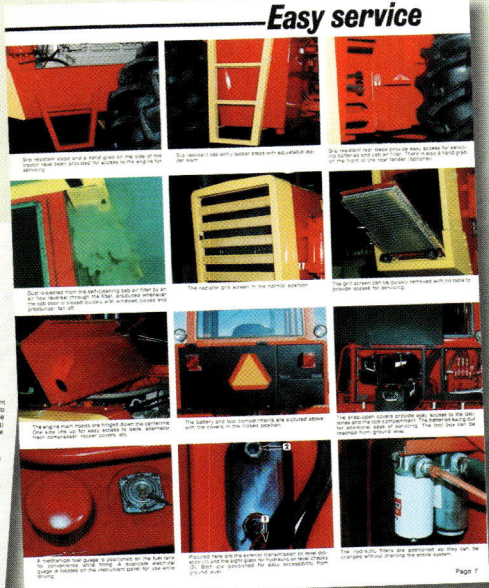

Above: Series 2 specifications explained in detail.

With the expanded facilities we were in a position to increase our production. We also needed more equipment for the tool room and the plant. The cutter bars were bent on a brake press and could only be made 15 feet long, and we were planning for 20-foot swathers. It was suggested that we get a roll former on which we could get a cutter bar of whatever length we wanted. We found a roll former near New York.

The popular 800 Series 2 of 1975 was typical of what supertractors had become, with its massive 13.9-litre Cummins engine with 235 hp. It had twelve forward speeds and a range of 2.6–14.3 mph. The turbocharged 825 and 850 had 250 hp and 280 hp respectively.

Versatile wins against farm implement kings

Pakosh is as heavy-duty as company's tractors

Top left: 1975 Annual Report.
Bottom left: Model 800 after a hard day's cultivating c.1975.
Right: *Winnipeg Free Press*, June 14, 1976.

Because of the heavy load on myself and Roy, we decided to hire people with managerial qualities. We found out that Ed Bell, who was a production manager of a large firm in Toronto, wanted to move out west, as he originally came from Neepawa. I was able to get his phone number and told him that we were looking for a general manager and that I'd be at Toronto on a certain date and would like to talk to him.

The 295-hp 900 model carried a Cummins V-903 V8 diesel. The turbocharged 950 was the largest at the time and had a 348-hp Cummins VT-903 V8 diesel engine.

Left: Versatile President Roy Robinson c.1976.
Centre: Versatile Chairman of the Board Peter Pakosh c.1976.
Right: Outside Fort Garry plant circa mid-1970s.

I'll never forget him saying, "If I take the job as a general manager of production I am not going to tell you how to design your equipment and you don't tell me how to make it." When I got home and told this to Roy, we both agreed that that's the man we're looking for. He flew down, and in a month's time he was back with his family renting a house and starting to work for Versatile.

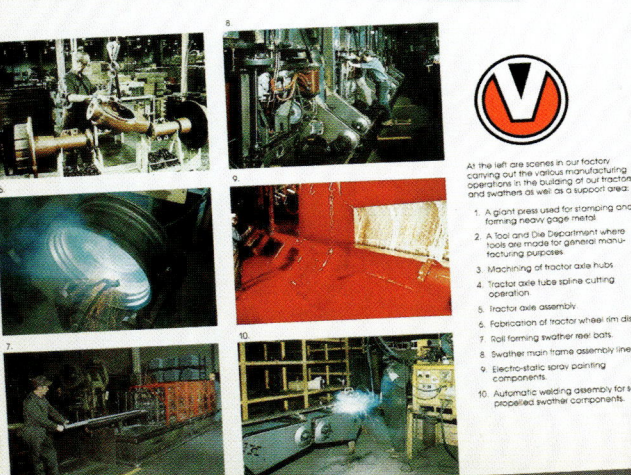

One man in the field could repair a Versatile transmission in four or five hours, whereas one competitor's similar machine required forty to sixty hours to repair the same transmission in a dealer's service bay. It was that simplicity of design that was the hallmark of all Versatile machines.

Top and bottom left: Inside production at the Fort Garry plant.
Right: Cutaway view of a Series 2 model 825.

This proved to be the best move we made, as he completely took over the production, buying the necessary machinery and organizing various department managers. It was relief to Roy and me.

This was also the year we built the new Parts Department. However, there is always something that comes up to complicate life.

By the late '70s, Versatile tractors accounted for 30 percent of the 200-plus horsepower sales in North America and continued to redefine the market with their simplicity of design. Roy Robinson once said: "To succeed in this business, you have to have the right idea at the right time and you must be able to anticipate what the farmers will need tomorrow," a feat definitely accomplished by Versatile.

Left: Model 1590 Versatile double-disc.
Top right: 348-hp model 950 c.1978.
Bottom right: M-10 pull-type swather.

We got news from our salesmen that Massey Harris bought our 145 tractor to copy. At the next sales meeting, I told them of the advice my boss had given me when I left M. H: "I wish you well, but always be innovative, never copy, because if you do he will find his mistakes first and always be ahead of you. Let someone else copy you and you will always stay ahead."

The Versatile bi-directional tractor

Back in the late 1960s, Peter's brother Dan had a simple idea. Why fit a loader on the front of a tractor when it would be far easier to mount it on the rear and swivel the operator around to work it? That simple idea lead Versatile to the development of the world's first bi-directional tractor, the Model 150.

Model 150

First offered in 1977, the Model 150 was referred to as a "push-pull" tractor and was marketed as being a "number of self-propelled machines in one."

Left: Versatile executives at the release of the first model 150 tractors c.1977.
Top right: Prototype of the bi-directional 150 before production.
Bottom right: The hydrostatic "Bi-di" 150 with snow blower.

We immediately decided to go to 700, 800 and 900 series of four-wheel-drive tractors, which put us way ahead of the market.

By 1972, the tool room required a lot of new equipment and had to be expanded into

a larger area. Special tools had to be made for a lot of the new tractor parts before we could go into production, as many of the assemblies had to be designed for volume production.

I t was sized and priced to compete with conventional two-wheel-drive tractors with similar horsepower and offered full-time hydrostatic drive to all four wheels, and articulated steering.

The 150 allowed farmers greater choice in connecting equipment and could achieve equal power whether using a push or pull implement. The bi-directional was truly "versatile." It was an instant success, and virtually overnight became the tractor for swathing, mowing and heavy swather work.

Top left: Model 150 promotional brochure c.1978.
Bottom left: Peter and Adeline at their 40th wedding anniversary.
Right: Need to use the rear attachment? Just spin around!

However, by mid-summer the production lines were ready, and production of the 700 and 900 models got underway.

In time, other models were added, such as the 800. Demand had been so great, especially in the '60s, that we had decided to build a plant in Fargo. The Fargo operation worked well. Some models of tractors were made there, especially the 800, where most of them were sold. Models 700 and 900 were made in Winnipeg.

Models 256 and 276

The 85-hp Model 256 replaced the Model 150 in 1984. The full bi-directional nature of the tractor was now realized by offering power takeoff, three-point linkage and remote hydraulic valves on both ends of the machine. The Model 276 "bi-di" followed a year later and delivered 100 hp at the PTO and thus could operate PTO-powered equipment comfortably, front and rear. Both models had full-time four-wheel-drive articulated frames and hydrostatic transmissions. In 1990, the 256 and 276 were replaced by the New Holland 9030.

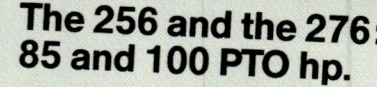

Left: Versatile 256 with multiple attachments at work.
Top right: Models 256 and 276 brochure c.1985.
Bottom right: Cummins powered 200 series bi-directionals.

Roy got Mike to build an eight-wheel-drive tractor that articulated the same way as the four-wheel. It was a monster. Mike named it "Big Roy." We never

went into production with it. It is now sitting at Austin Museum in Manitoba, where they show it every year during the threshing reunion using old threshing machines.

TV140

New Holland continued the tradition and brought Dan out of retirement to help update the tractor for the next century. Although the basics remained the same, practically the whole tractor was modernized, from new mechanical and transmission changes to a larger and more comfortable cab and controls that now turned with the operator. The TV140 was released in 1998.

Top left: New Holland bi-directional TV140 c.2000.
Bottom left: Ford New Holland 9030 c.1990s.
Right: Front and back of the bi-directional 9030.

Most of the other parts outlets were put in place.

Operating the two plants, Fargo and Winnipeg, was not an easy job. We did, however, put together a good group of sales and production personnel. It took time to integrate the two operations. The orders for the next year's production were very heavy, as we already had about 12 salesmen and about 500 dealers, so it was necessary again to reorganize the two plants in order to meet the production schedule.

Big Roy

It was Roy Robinson who decided to put Versatile ahead of the field by building a giant tractor, one that could outperform anything else on the market with ease. The instruction to the design team was simple—build the world's biggest tractor.

The result was the 26-ton, 600-hp, eight-wheel-drive Versatile 1080. At the factory, they affectionately called it Big Roy. This prairie monster had a 19-litre Cummins engine in the rear, while the front section held the massive 2,100-litre fuel tank.

Big Roy proved easy to drive, but because of its enormous size was very hard to maneuver.

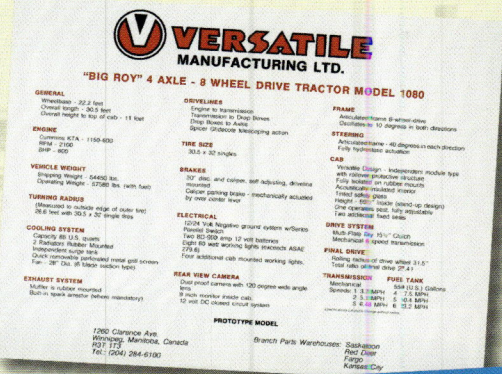

Left: Versatile's 600-hp model 1080 in field test.
Top right: Big Roy's impressive specifications.
Bottom right: Promotional pamphlets created much excitement.

Nineteen seventy-four was an international year. Enquiries were made about the need for tractors in Britain, Europe, Russia, Australia, and Africa. The findings were that there was a good market for four-wheel-drive tractors, but of smaller size. So the engineering group went to work and designed Model 300 and also bi-directional Model 150, now 256. It wasn't long before the design was complete, and soon these models went into production.

Rear visibility was almost completely blocked because the engine was mounted extra high to clear the axles and allow space for the eight-wheel-drive transmission drivelines. So a closed-circuit TV with a camera on the back had to be installed. The operator could thus see either a general rear view for reversing or could tilt the camera down to position the drawbar correctly to attach implements.

The new tractor caused a sensation, but due to soaring development costs, along with the fact that there were no implements big enough at the time to challenge its pulling power, Versatile eventually decided to cancel the Big Roy program.

Top: The 8WD Big Roy demonstrating its tremendous pulling power.
Bottom left: Parked outside Versatile's Fort Garry plant.
Bottom right: Advertisement for one of the many Big Roy appearances.

Big Roy is still on display at the Manitoba Agricultural Museum in Austin, Manitoba, Canada.

In 1975 Mom and I went to Algeria in regards to 300 tractors of Model 700 that were sold to them. I provided them with service procedures. Earlier that year we had a visit by the Polish ambassador from Ottawa. He wanted to know more about Versatile and about the possibility of doing some business with Poland.

Satisfied with their accomplishments, and now at retirement age, Versatile co-founders Peter Pakosh and Roy Robinson decided to sell their stake in the company and retire. What they had built from that backyard in Toronto some thirty years earlier was truly remarkable. Versatile grew from selling ten grain augers per year from a basement shop to a multinational farm-equipment manufacturer with annual sales in excess of $100 million. It grew from 50 staff to over 1,300 employees, and grew from salesmen driving from one small prairie town to the next selling farm implements to having a network of over 2,000 dealers.

Top: 12 numbered model 850s all bought by the Kalcevic family.
Bottom left: Versatile rig pulling out to deliver parts.
Bottom right: Peter and Roy accepting the Industrial Development Award c.1977.

He introduced to us Ursus Tractor Co. in Warsaw and wondered if we would be interested in a trading deal on parts with Ursus Tractor Co. I told him that a Versatile group was planning to visit Poland this year and possibly negotiate some trading of at least components for our tractors.

His eyes just lit up.

7

CHANGING HANDS—THE END OF AN ERA

Versatile Cornat Corporation

After a failed attempt by Hesston International to acquire Versatile in 1976, Cornat Industries of Vancouver, British Columbia, bought majority share of the company. The late '70s saw new models released, and in an effort to penetrate the lucrative corn and soybean row-crop market, a new tractor, adapted for row crops, was released. It was the Versatile 500.

Left: Row crop model 500 poster c.1977.
Centre: Model 500 busy cultivating.
Right: *Versatile News* of March 1977 announces sale.

I also told him that I would like to follow up the history of our parents, who were located near Maczejowa, not far from Krakow.

We made arrangements to travel on a Versatile visa as businessmen.

More new models would follow in 1977 with the release of a new series of tractors with "constant power," another first in the farm-equipment industry. The new models were the 835, 855, 875 and 935 and had a range of 230–330 hp. With these models, the company added black to its traditional red-and-yellow paint scheme.

At this time, Versatile also established its first overseas subsidiary, in Australia.

Left: Versatile 875 with new colour scheme c.1978.
Top right: Model 400 swather (with cab) outside factory.
Bottom right: 1977 Annual Report.

When we arrived in Warsaw we got a royal treatment. Customs were instructed to let us through without checking our baggage.

Our first trip was to make contact with the Ursus Tractor people to make it official. After a couple of days we headed to Maczejowa and got in touch with the town hall to get information as to where the original property of the Pakosz family was located.

In 1979 Versatile opened its global market even further by reaching an agreement with Fiat to supply its four-wheel-drive tractors to the European market. The Fiat Versatile tractors were offered in four engine sizes and still bore the Versatile name and logo—the 230-hp Fiat 44-23, the 280-hp 44-28, the 330-hp 44-33 and the 350-hp 44-55.

MODEL 480 FIELD SPRAYER

Modern technology, engineering, and Versatile have developed, through the latest research, testing, and design methods, the revolutionary Model 480 field sprayer. The Model 480 sprayer gives Versatile the most economical and efficient sprayer of its type.

The Model 480 sprayer is designed to give maximum performance and operator convenience to allow for larger areas of acre coverage in less time.

Seconds is all it takes to swing the boom from transport to field position, and no tools are required. The entire boom height can also be adjusted in seconds without tools, while maintaining a constant spray angle at any height. Loosening a bolt for each boom section is all it takes to adjust the spray angle.

A tandem walking beam type undercarriage assures a long life of the sprayer components. In addition, a tandem boom support system with caster wheels, increases stability of the booms.

Seven indexed settings can be chosen through the use of the special selector valve, with immediate response in starting or stopping flow to the three section boom. Controls and valves are mounted on a slit-telescopic mast that can be adjusted for easy accessibility from the tractor seat.

The Model 480 has a tank capacity of 400 Imperial gallons (480 U.S. gallons), with choice area coverage of 67 feet, or 80 feet (with 6 foot coverage offset nozzles).

Designed to conserve on costly chemicals, the spray tips on the Versatile sprayers provide an 80 degree fan angle. This allows a lower boom setting and reduces the possibilities of wind drift, which wastes chemicals as well as damages crop or foliage. Stainless steel spray tips, which maintain their original spray angle much longer than brass tips, are another chemical saving feature. Because of wearing, the fan angle on a brass tip narrows, and the operator is forced to set the booms at a higher position, letting the opportunity of spray drift occur. Each nozzle also has a built in check valve to prevent drip when the pump is stopped.

More acres per hour through higher field speeds is now possible, with the high capacity PTO operated pump. The pump has reserve capacity, to ensure proper agitation of the materials in the tank.

To ensure more hours of productivity in the fields, Versatile sprayers are built with easy servicing in mind. A quick release, line filter can be removed by hand and cleaned in seconds. A two inch drain located in the tank sump, allows unused spray materials to flush water to be drained quickly from the tank.

The Model 480 field sprayer is one of the ways Versatile has shown that it understands the growing and changing trends of today's farming needs. A traditionally superior sprayer that covers many acres at an economical price; and still maintains its durability. Another example of **GOOD VALUE** by **VERSATILE**.

VERSATILE
MANUFACTURING LTD.

Top left: Fiat Versatile model 44-28 c.1979.
Bottom left: The Fiat models still bore the Versatile logo.
Right: Model 480 sprayer advertisement c.1980.

The clerk was very cooperative and drove us down to the property where my grandfather and father were born. He also showed us where the Wrona property was. It was an interesting sight.

In Warsaw I went to meet the Ursus people for further discussion; however, nothing developed, but the president gave me his business card so that I could prove that we were there on business officially, which was of great help in the event someone stopped us for questioning.

By 1980 the company adopted a new logo to reflect its broader business interests. Testifying to the respect Versatile had garnered over the years, the company also adopted a new slogan, "We've Got a Name to Live Up to."

MODEL 10 PULL-TYPE SWATHERS BY VERSATILE

FAMOUS FOR ENGINEERED QUALITY AND DEPENDABILITY

DOUBLE OFFSET TANDEM DISC

MODEL 1609–1610

VERSATILE
MANUFACTURING LTD.

Left: The 348-hp model 950 was Versatile's largest at the time.
Top right: Model 10 pull-type swather ad c.1980.
Bottom right: Model 1609–1610 disc ad c.1980.

After a few days we flew to Moscow on the pretense that Versatile was interested in doing business with Belarus Tractor, located outside of Moscow. They drove us down to the plant and showed us their production line of tractors.

They indicated that they were interested but needed to talk about it. A year later Roy and Rose flew down to Moscow via London but nothing happened.

One of Versatile's popular models in the early '80s was the 555, or, as many farmers call it, the "Triple Nickel." Built in 1980, the 555 had a 555-ci Cummins V8 diesel engine, producing 210 hp. Its manual transmission had fifteen forward-speed gears but no power shift.

Left: Versatile Corporation brochure c.1981.
Top right: A 210-hp model 555 or "Triple Nickel" working hard.
Bottom right: Versatile's slogan for the eighties: "We've got a name to live up to."

The year 1976 proved to be our best production year so far, both in Winnipeg and Fargo. We increased production on all

our equipment. The demand was heavy, especially in the U.S.

Also introduced was the Trans-axial 2000 pull-type combine, as well as the new SP4400 swather.

A multi-million-dollar plant expansion came in 1981 and allowed production of new tractor models ranging from 71 hp to 470 hp. The new-look Series 3 Versatiles had a wide band of yellow, orange and black on the side of the engine hood and cab.

Top: Versatile's impressive line-up of powerful tractors c.1981.
Bottom left: A Series 3 model 975 with new colour scheme c.1982.
Bottom right: Models SP4400 and SP400 swather manual c.1982.

Financially, this was the best year for Versatile. The stock went up to $20 a share. In 1963, when we went public, it had started at $5 a share.

One day Lyle Yost of Hesston Manufacturing (we met him at EMI Chicago) phoned and said that he would like to talk to us about merging or buying out Versatile outright.

Above: A 470-hp Versatile model 1150 in field photos c.1983.

Most noteworthy was the 470-hp articulated Versatile 1150 with power-shift transmission. Electronic selection of twelve forward speeds and two reverse allowed the operator to select speeds on the go without lifting implements.

The Designation 6 Versatile models, 836, 856, 876, 936, 956, 976, were introduced in October 1984 for the 1985 model year. The Versatile engineers gave the new models from 210-to-360-engine horsepower, along with a bold new look.

Roy and I went to see him in Hesston, Kansas, and talked things over. We told him that we would sell. But in Canada we had in Ottawa a Foreign Investment Review Agency (FIRA) which would have to authorize the sale. Lyle had a jet and said, "I will fly to Winnipeg, pick you up and fly to Ottawa to see FIRA to get permission for the sale." However, they refused, so we all went home.

The 800 Series were both fuel efficient and durable. They featured a leaner 10-litre, 611-ci Cummins Constant Power in-line 6-cylinder diesel turbocharged engine with 10 percent better fuel efficiency than previous comparable engines. They were also available with easy-to-adjust row-crop axles, a 1,000-rpm PTO and high-clearance 42-inch tires.

Left: Designation 6 model 756 demonstrating pulling power c.1985.
Top right: Peter with great-granddaughter behind Big Roy.
Bottom right: Series 3 model 1150 kicking up some dust.

In the fall of this year we were contacted by Cornat Industries of Vancouver, who were interested in buying Versatile. It was OK because it was a Canadian company, and we did not have to go through FIRA. A deal was made for settlement on January 8, 1977.

opular on farms because of its size was the 900 Series, which included the Ford Versatile 976, with its 855-ci Cummins in-line 6-cylinder turbocharged diesel engine. The Designation 6 models were the first to introduce Versatile's new closed centre-load-sensing hydraulic system and the labour-saving twelve-speed powershift transmissions. Other models, such as the 756, 846 and 946, would follow in later years.

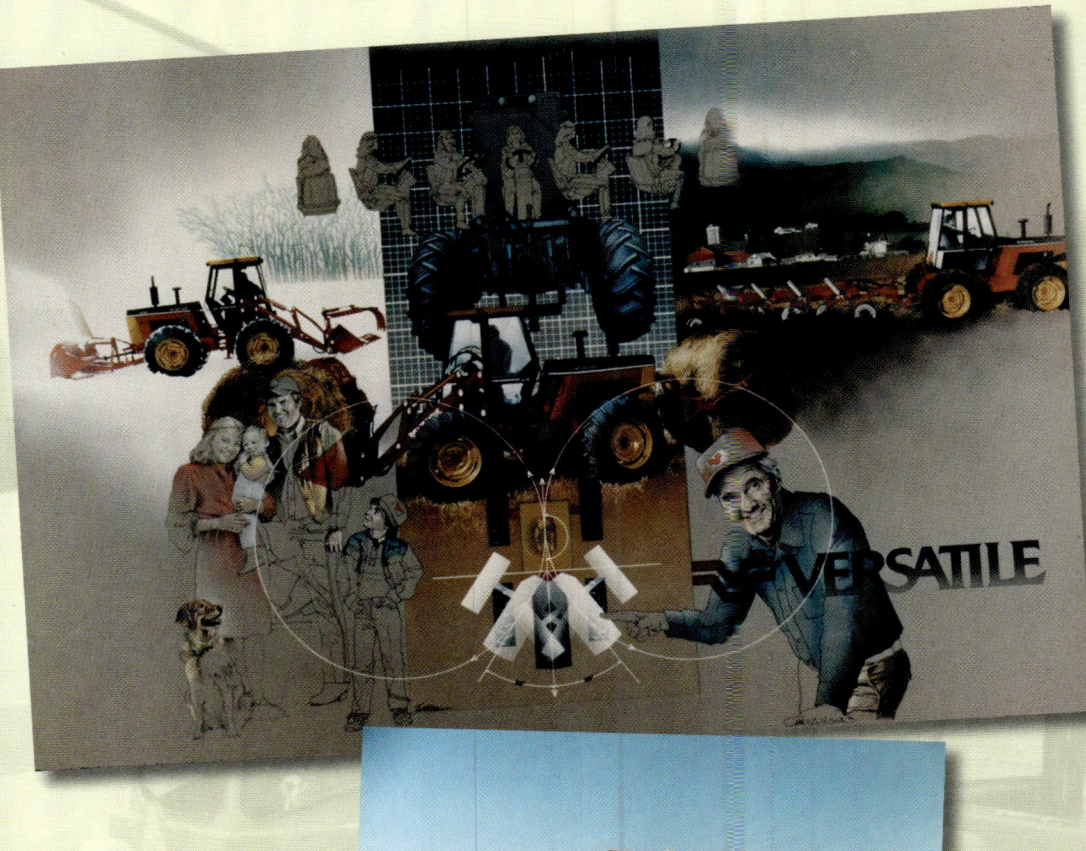

Left: Test 4WD self-propelled Trans-Axial combine c.1984.
Top right: Versatile promotional poster c.1984.
Bottom right: Trans Axial 2000 pull-type combine built by Peter and Dan.

We had a regular meeting of the shareholders in 1977 at a place downtown, as there were at least 500 shareholders that

showed up. Of those present and the proxy vote, the majority were in favor to accept the deal, as it was a good offer. It worked out well for all of us.

Ford New Holland

With 1987 came the end of an era. The Versatile Manufacturing Company of Winnipeg, Manitoba, and the Sperry New Holland Company in Pennsylvania were acquired by the Ford Tractor Division. The new company was renamed Ford New Holland.

Left: Working copy of Versatile 4400 swather ad c.1985.
Centre: Designation 6 model 836 in field c.1986.
Right: *Winnipeg Free Press*, February 18, 1987.

On January 8, Roy and I got one share each for $1 just to see what these certificates were going to look like. I have a framed copy on my desk. We got cheques for the balance, which we put in the bank. Most of the other shareholders stayed in, but Roy and I decided to get out completely. After this, it was back to work for Roy and me, but for a new management team.

New Holland North America

In 1993 Fiat acquired the remaining shares of Ford New Holland and changed the name to simply New Holland. Part of the purchase agreement required Fiat to keep the Ford name on the tractors until January 1, 2000. With this change, New Holland emerged as a leader in four-wheel drives and also continued to recognize the Versatile tradition by including the name on its product.

Top left: Ford New Holland 80 Series Versatile brochure c.1995.
Top right: Beautiful overhead view of a 300-hp Versatile 9480.
Bottom: 1995 line-up 250-hp 9280, 300-hp 9480 and 400-hp 9880.

In 1986 Cornat Industries started to get themselves in trouble at Versatile. They started to realize that maybe they had taken a bigger bite than they could chew. Peter Paul Saunders, who was the president of Cornat, started to make it known that they would be interested to sell Versatile.

The new Versatiles were sleeker, more ergonomic and bigger than ever. First off the line was the Versatile 80 Series. The smallest was the 9280 and had a 10-litre, 611-ci Cummins 250-hp turbo.

Next, fitted with 14-litre, 855-ci turbo-intercooled Cummins, were the 300-hp 9480, the 350-hp 9680 and the 400-hp 9880. These three bigger models held 245 gallons of fuel, 16 gallons of coolant and the axles needed 12.7 gallons of coolant. They were also available with triples as an option.

Left: Versatile built the biggest and best tractors.
Right: Close-up of a Ford New Holland Versatile 9680.

John Deere was the first to want to buy Versatile, but it was Ford who got into the picture and started to show interest in Versatile, after having already bought New Holland. For some time there was a lot of activity, as Ford New Holland did not know if they alone could handle it, as the company had grown about four times in size since when New Holland first wanted to buy us out in 1961.

Even higher-horsepower models were released in the mid-'90s with the 82 Series. The model 9282 had 260 hp, 9482 had 310 hp, 9682 had 360 hp and the 9882 had 425 hp. The newer models had more hydraulic flow, more cab comfort and were easier than ever to service, with flip-up engine shielding and sight gauges.

Top left: One of the last New Hollands with the name Versatile.
Bottom left: New Holland 82 Series brochure c.1995.
Right: Peter's last visit during the New Holland years c.1997.

Years later, Fiat became interested in buying Versatile. They found out that Ford's Farm Equipment Division was considering closing down the farm division and just concentrating on the manufacturing of automobiles. They got in touch with the Farm Division executives and suggested that they should get together and buy out Versatile, as they had the best four-wheel-drive tractor on the market.

Bühler Versatile Inc.

The year 2000 was a historic one as New Holland merged with Case and formed CNH Global. The Versatile name and original Clarence Avenue plant was then sold to Bühler Industries Inc. of Winnipeg, Manitoba, Canada, and Versatile again became independent.

Left: Versatile, red and yellow again.
Top right: The new line of Versatile 4WD and Genesis.
Bottom right: Bühler Versatile Genesis brochure c.2002.

Ford only had a two-wheel-drive and some small equipment, as Henry Ford was farm oriented and always wanted to do something for the farm industry. I do not know how and who did the negotiating, but I believe for a while that Ford stayed in the background so that New Holland could work out at the best deal possible.

Equipment Manufacturers Institute (EMI)

The Equipment Manufacturers Institute (now the Association of Equipment Manufacturers) is recognized around the world as the oldest and largest trade association for the manufacture of agricultural, construction and forestry equipment. In celebration of the existence of the institute during the period 1893–1993, when so many contributed so much to the mechanization of agriculture and construction, EMI chose at its centennial convention to identify and honour one hundred significant contributions and contributors that it believed merited special attention for benefits bestowed upon mankind in the pursuit of food, shelter and mobility.

Top left: Don, Jarrod, Peter and Ken Pakosh at EMI 100th Annual Convention.
Bottom left: Peter reminisces at the Massey Harris display.
Right: The Fairmont Hotel ballroom in Chicago, Illinois.

All the Ford implement dealers and all the New Holland implement dealers were now also Versatile dealers. As soon as possible a new paint shop was set up to automatically paint blue as they moved along the line.

At EMI's first convention in 1894, sixteen "pioneers" were recognized for their achievements, including famous men like Jerome I. Case, John Deere, Cyrus Hall McCormack and James Oliver. Henry Ford received the honour for contributing greatly to the transition to power farming in the early 1900s. And Peter Pakosh also was among those recognized at that event on September 27, 1993, at the Fairmont Hotel in Chicago, Illinois. Accompanied by his two sons, Ken and Don, and his grandson, Jarrod, Peter shared the stage with the greatest names to have ever advanced and innovated the industry.

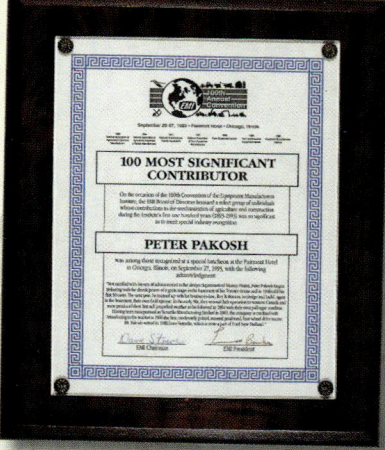

Top left: Peter with his grandson, Jarrod, after receiving his award.
Bottom left: The Pakosh family still working their land.
Right: Peter Pakosh's EMI "100 Most Significant Contributors" award.

At Kendon, I started to work on a self-unloading hopper that would hydraulically unload the hopper by tilting. I only made one. I tested it on Ted Campeau's farm and then took it to my brother Ed's farm in Saskatchewan.

About the middle of August, Roy and Rose flew to Freeport, Bahamas, where Roy got very sick. He went to Rands Hospital, where he died on August 30. It was a terrible setback.

Honourary Citizen of the City of Winnipeg

EMI called Peter Pakosh "an agricultural equipment design pioneer of great foresight," and Versatile the "commercializer" of four-wheel-drive tractors in North America. At that same convention, Peter was also named an Honourary Citizen of the City of Winnipeg for his hard work and dedication that had benefitted that city so greatly.

Left: Peter was also named Honourary Citizen of the city of Winnipeg at the event.
Centre: The Pakosh boys during City ceremony.
Right: *Winnipeg Free Press* excerpt highlighted Peter's lifelong faith c.1976.

In September 1993, Ken, Don, Jarrod and I all went to the EMI Award Convention in Chicago. It was really a thrilling experience for all of us, especially Jarrod, as he had never seen anything like this.

Jehovah's Witness

He favors suspenders and dark, rectangular suits of the sort associated with superannuated members of the Soviet politboro. In conversation, he'll hitch at his trousers and make loud, phlegm-clearing sounds in his throat as if he were out kicking clods in the back 40.

But, more than anything that establishes him as a curious iconoclast of the local business elite, there's his religion. He's a Jehovah's Witness and an elder in his church at that.

And, so is Roy Robinson, who is his brother-in-law, long-time partner and Versatile president. So is Jacke Eckmire, Versatile secretary-treasurer and vice-president. Other executives and "about 50 or 60" workers at Versatile's Fort Garry plant are also Witnesses.

This isn't to suggest fundamentalism and corporate capitalism are necessarily antithetical, strange bedfellows though they may be. But, to understand the vaunted reputation and vaulting growth of Versatile, it must be within the context of the Witnesses' view of the market-place.

Weekend piety and business as usual the rest of the week aren't part of it. Secular and spiritual conduct are inseparable. Work is purifying. But, most of all, their moral code — which makes c l e a r distinctions between material comfort and love of materialism, use of money and love of money — precludes corner cutting, indifferent production, sharp practice of any kind.

When a Versatile tractor or swather comes off the line, it might be said, quality control is guarnateed by an authority higher than industry regulations.

No compromising

"We simply live and work according to biblical standards of decency," Peter Pakosh explains. "We're dedicated to giving a full day's work and we respect moral obligations. We aren't about to compromise our convictions just to make money. Versatile succeeded," he stresses, "through hard work and plain honesty."

Completing technical school, Pakosh took further engineering classes at night school and, in 1940, moved east, landing a job as a draftsman in the tool department of what was then Massey-Harris.

"I was full of ideas. I wanted to design farm machinery in their engineering design department." Improperly qualified, he pursued the job. He was constantly rebuffed.

Versatile Founders' Boardroom

In 1997 Peter and his family returned to the Versatile plant on Clarence Avenue in Winnipeg that he had founded some forty years earlier. On that occasion, New Holland saw fit to recognize both Peter and Roy for their accomplishments, and named a newly renovated boardroom in their honour. The "Founders" boardroom is still there today, right where it all began.

Left: New Holland's boardroom dedication in Winnipeg c.1997.
Top right: Versatile 5000 combine still running great in Saskatchewan.
Bottom right: Peter, at age 86, would still spend 8-hour days cultivating.

I was so happy for the privilege of being present with two sons and a grandson and being honoured with being named one of the one hundred most significant contributors to mechanization of equipment. That same night, I also received the Honourary Citizenship Award from the City of Winnipeg. What an honour to be recognized for all those hard years of sweat and tears.

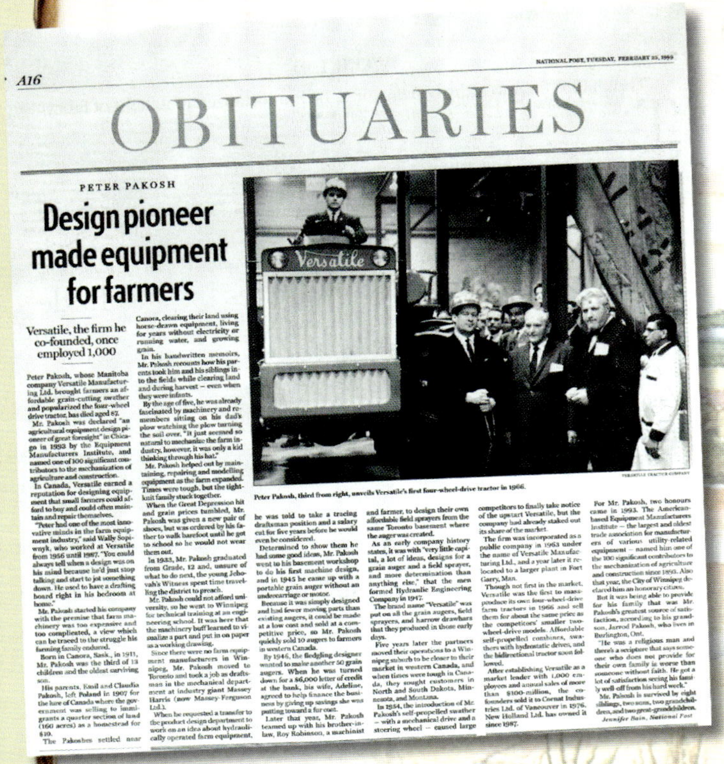

A16

NATIONAL POST, TUESDAY, FEBRUARY 23, 1999

OBITUARIES

PETER PAKOSH

Design pioneer made equipment for farmers

Versatile, the firm he co-founded, once employed 1,000

Peter Pakosh, whose Manitoba company Versatile Manufacturing Ltd. brought farmers an affordable grain-cutting swather and popularized the four-wheel drive tractor, has died aged 87.

Mr. Pakosh was declared "an agricultural equipment design pioneer of great foresight" in Chicago in 1993 by the Equipment Manufacturers Institute, and named one of 100 significant contributors to the mechanization of agriculture and construction.

In Canada, Versatile earned a reputation for designing equipment that small farmers could afford to buy and could often maintain and repair themselves.

"Peter had one of the most innovative minds in the farm equipment industry," said Wally Sopiwnyk, who worked at Versatile from 1956 until 1987. "You could always tell when a design was on his mind because he'd just stop talking and start to jot something down. He used to have a drafting board right in his bedroom at home."

Mr. Pakosh started his company with the premise that farm machinery was too expensive and too complicated, a view which can be traced to the struggle his farming family endured.

Born in Canora, Sask., in 1911, Mr. Pakosh was the third of 13 children and the oldest surviving son.

His parents, Emil and Claudia Pakosh, left Poland in 1907 for the lure of Canada where the government was selling to immigrants a quarter section of land (160 acres) as a homestead for $10.

The Pakoshes settled near Canora, clearing their land using horse-drawn equipment, living for years without electricity or running water, and growing grain.

In his handwritten memoirs, Mr. Pakosh recounts how his parents took him and his siblings into the fields while clearing land and during harvest — even when they were infants.

By the age of five, he was already fascinated by machinery and remembers sitting on his dad's plow watching the plow turning the soil over. "It just seemed so natural to mechanize the farm industry, however, it was only a kid thinking through his hat."

Mr. Pakosh helped out by maintaining, repairing and modelling equipment as the farm expanded. Times were tough, but the tight-knit family stuck together.

When the Great Depression hit and grain prices tumbled, Mr. Pakosh was given a new pair of shoes, but was ordered by his father to walk barefoot until he got to school so he would not wear them out.

In 1933, Mr. Pakosh graduated from Grade, 12 and, unsure of what to do next, the young Jehovah's Witness spent time travelling the district to preach.

Mr. Pakosh could not afford university, so he went to Winnipeg for technical training at an engineering school. It was here that the machinery buff learned to visualize a part and put in on paper as a working drawing.

Since there were no farm equipment manufacturers in Winnipeg, Mr. Pakosh moved to Toronto and took a job as draftsman in the mechanical department at industry giant Massey Harris (now Massey-Ferguson Ltd.).

When he requested a transfer to the product design department to work on an idea about hydraulically operated farm equipment, he was told to take a tracing draftsman position and a salary cut for five years before he would even be considered.

Determined to show them he had some good ideas, Mr. Pakosh went to his basement workshop to do his first machine design, and in 1945 he came up with a portable grain auger without an undercarriage or motor.

Because it was simply designed and had fewer moving parts than existing augers, it could be made at a low cost and sold at a competitive price, so Mr. Pakosh quickly sold 10 augers to farmers in western Canada.

By 1946, the fledgling designer wanted to make another 50 grain augers. When he was turned down for a $6,000 letter of credit at the bank, his wife, Adeline, agreed to help finance the business by giving up savings she was putting toward a fur coat.

Later that year, Mr. Pakosh teamed up with his brother-in-law, Roy Robinson, a machinist and farmer, to design their own affordable field sprayers from the same Toronto basement where the auger was created.

As an early company history states, it was with "very little capital, a lot of ideas, designs for a grain auger and a field sprayer, and more determination than anything else," that the men formed Hydraulic Engineering Company in 1947.

The brand name "Versatile" was put on all the grain augers, field sprayers, and harrow drawbars that they produced in those early days.

Five years later the partners moved their operations to a Winnipeg suburb to be closer to their market in western Canada, and when times were tough in Canada, they sought customers in North and South Dakota, Minnesota, and Montana.

In 1954, the introduction of Mr. Pakosh's self-propelled swather — with a mechanical drive and a steering wheel — caused large competitors to finally take notice of the upstart Versatile, but the company had already staked out its share of the market.

The firm was incorporated as a public company in 1963 under the name of Versatile Manufacturing Ltd., and a year later it relocated to a larger plant in Fort Garry, Man.

Though not first in the market, Versatile was the first to mass-produce its own four-wheel-drive farm tractors in 1966 and sell them for about the same price as the competitors' smaller two-wheel-drive models. Affordable self-propelled combines, swathers with hydrostatic drives, and the bidirectional tractor soon followed.

After establishing Versatile as a market leader with 1,000 employees and annual sales of more than $100-million, the co-founders sold it to Cornat Industries Ltd. of Vancouver in 1976. New Holland Ltd. has owned it since 1987.

For Mr. Pakosh, two honours came in 1993. The American-based Equipment Manufacturers Institute — the largest and oldest trade association for manufacturers of various utility-related equipment — named him one of the 100 significant contributors to the mechanization of agriculture and construction since 1893. Also that year, the City of Winnipeg declared him an honorary citizen.

But it was being able to provide for his family that was Mr. Pakosh's greatest source of satisfaction, according to his grandson, Jarrod Pakosh, who lives in Burlington, Ont.

"He was a religious man and there's a scripture that says someone who does not provide for their own family is worse than someone without faith. He got a lot of satisfaction seeing his family well-off from his hard work."

Mr. Pakosh is survived by eight siblings, two sons, two grandchildren, and two great-grandchildren.

Jennifer Bain, National Post

Peter Pakosh, third from right, unveils Versatile's first four-wheel-drive tractor in 1966.

VERSATILE TRACTOR COMPANY

The following year we all went to my brother Ed's and did some grain hauling. I'll never forget how Lisa was able to handle the 800 tractor, pulling a load of grain. Ken, Don and Jarrod also drove the small tractor and the truck. Ed sure appreciated the help. I got a kick out of Lynn driving the half-ton truck. I was surprised how she could handle it. She even took me for a drive. Don also was of great help. We all got a kick out of this trip. I will never forget Lynn and Lisa raking in front of the old house to get it ready for viewing. Everyone appreciated seeing the old place again, especially those of us who were brought up there.

Back in Winnipeg we visited Versatile. We have a stack of pictures, but I only put in a couple. It was a very interesting tour of the plant. It sure is changed from my days, but there are still a lot of my original designs.

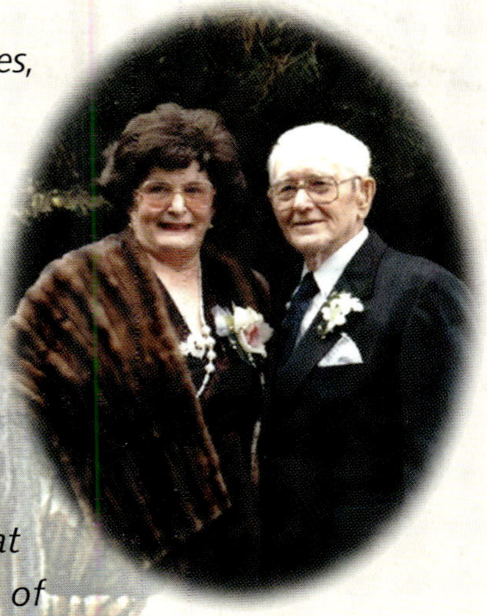

The year 1995 was the worst of my life. Nanny's health kept failing and she died on April 14 at sundown (Memorial Day). What a shock to all. Nanny lived a life of dignity and died in dignity, now awaiting resurrection. Funeral arrangements had to be made, and she was buried on April 19, at Elgin Mills Cemetery in Toronto.

Jarrod and Lisa's baby's name is Keana. Nanny would have just adored her.

It's been a tough life, but I wouldn't change a thing. I think back over the years and am proud of what we were able to accomplish. It was always my dream, even as a boy, to improve and innovate farming for the average farmer, and that's exactly what we did at Versatile. But most important to me is the principle in 1 Timothy 5:8, that he who does not provide for his family is worse than a person without faith. Grampa's very happy that I was able to do that for my family.

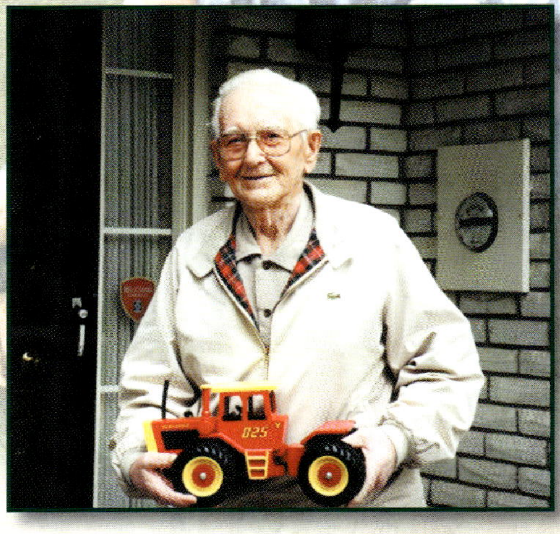

Peter Pakosh died "old and satisfied with days" on February 20, 1999.

Left: The *National Post*, February 23, 1999.
Centre: Peter holds up a Versatile model 825 toy tractor c.1998.
Right: Peter and Adeline Pakosh at their grandson's wedding c.1991.

9

MARKETING A WINNER

Farm-equipment manufacturing has always been one of the most competitive markets in the world, and farm-equipment companies know the importance of developing loyalty to both their brand and their colours.

Throughout its history, Versatile received many awards for its original and dynamic ad campaigns. Here are a few pages that demonstrate how Versatile attracted business and wooed farmers through effective marketing.

DEFENSIVE ACTION

CONSTANT POWER
VERSATILE
MANUFACTURING COMPANY

POWER UP

Hockey great Bobby Hull takes delivery.

CONSTANT POWER
FOUR-WHEEL-DRIVE TRACTORS

by **VERSATILE**

Built for each other—Versatile and Constant Power

New Constant Power engines furnish the muscle Versatile tractors deliver it. It's the working reliability and high performance combination you demand — and **get** from the Versatile Constant Power team.

Four models harness this new breed of engine — from the hefty 230 hp Model 835 to the acre-eating 330 hp Model 935.

Versatile teams the toughest with the newest:

Versatile tractors have a solid reputation for rugged field performance with minimum downtime. Now, with Constant Power engines they're even tougher to beat. When tough field spots or hills are encountered, rpm's drop, but torque rises to maintain nearly uniform horsepower through the operating range. You forge ahead without shifting down. With that kind of lugging ability, you have the power reserve to be more productive without investing in a larger engine or an expensive powershift transmission.

Versatile tractors deliver that power efficiently:

The Versatile-designed transmission combines both range and gear speeds in one unit for minimal horsepower loss and greater reliability. Plus a heavy duty drive train that puts the power to the wheels with less horsepower loss than most other 4 WDs on the market. And when you consider that Versatile tractors are built for easy maintenance and fast servicing you know you've got a tractor that's always ready to work when you are.

Cab comfort keeps you working as productively as your Versatile:

You'll best appreciate Versatile performance from the air conditioned cab. Other standard features include a tilt-telescopic steering column, AM-FM radio, thick foam acoustic insulation, and a fully adjustable Grammer seat.

Versatile and Constant Power. For greater productivity and proven dependability it's the only combination to consider.

Only Model 875 for sale in Nebraska

VERSATILE
MANUFACTURING COMPANY
A DIVISION OF VERSATILE CORNAT CORPORATION

For information contact:
Head Office: 1260 Clarence Ave., Winnipeg, Canada R3T 1T3 Tel: (204) 284-6100

At one point in its storied past, Versatile was coveted by John Deere, Agco and Hesston International, while Ford, New Holland and Fiat all played ownership roles in the plant. Today, Versatile is alive and well under the ownership of Bühler Versatile Inc. Versatile has indeed claimed its place in history, and will always be a name to live up to, both in the tractor world and on farms across the globe. For over a half century, Versatile truly has been "a farm boy's dream."